A Sheep In Wolf's Clothing

Also by Denise Noe

Hard Copy Books

The Complete Married... with Children Book: TV's Dysfunctional Family Phenomenon

Teletubbies On the Screen and Behind the Scenes

Christmas Gifts from the Chanukah Crowd: The Extraordinary Contributions of Americans Jews to Christmas

Maury: The Story of an American Pop Culture Institution

Wishbone Behind the Scenes

The Bloodied and the Broken

Justice Gone Haywire

I Spy, You Spy, They Spy

Ebook-Only Books by Denise Noe

Suffer Little Children

Obsessions & Exorcisms in the Work of Joyce Carol Oates

Voices from the Inside: Letters from Famous Prisoners

A Sheep In Wolf's Clothing

The Life of Marie Windsor

by Denise Noe

BearManor Media

2023

Published in the United States of America by:

BearManor Media
1317 Edgewater Dr #110
Orlando FL 32804

bearmanormedia.com

Printed in the United States.

Typesetting and layout by John Teehan

ISBN—979-8-88771-066-2

Table of Contents

Author's Note

THE PURPOSE OF THIS BOOK is to relate the rich and accomplished life of Marie Windsor, an actress who added immeasurably to the entertainment industry through her work. In discussing films in which Marie appeared, it has sometimes been necessary to relate the entire plot and include a discussion of the film's ending. However, in cases in which the author believes that the reader can get a good idea of the vehicle in which Marie appeared and the contribution she made to it without "giving the game away," I have discussed the start of the story but left much out so readers who have not seen that particular film or TV show will be able to enjoy the surprises it might contain.

Although Marie Windsor is best known today for her depictions of femme fatale characters in motion pictures usually called film noir, she played just about every type of character in just about every type of film and television show. She was in many Westerns. In discussing Westerns, I sometimes use the term "American Indian" or "Indian" since this was the term used for indigenous Americans in the films themselves as well as during the contemporary period in which they were made. No offense is intended to the people who got to this continent so much earlier than other racial/ethnic groups. I personally use "Native American" or "indigenous Americans" but found such terms unwieldy and awkward when applied to motion pictures crafted when "Indian" was the term within the movie itself as well as in discussions and reviews of said movie. It is my sincere hope that Native American readers will understand that no offense is meant to them whatsoever.

I want to thank Marie Windsor's son, Rick Hupp, for his cooperation in the writing of this book. Without that cooperation, it is unlikely it would have been written. I give him my sincere thanks.

Emily Marie Grows Up In Marysvale

MARY IS ONE OF THE MOST popular names for females in the Western world, largely because the name is that of one of its most pivotal female figures, the Virgin Mary. It is likely those who founded a small town in Utah they named Marysvale had "Mother of God" in mind when they named the town. A Marysvale town existed since the late 19th century as demonstrated by the fact that a Marysvale post office is known to have operated since 1872. The general area had often been a place of mining as silver ores were found in the 1860s, gold in 1889, and uranium in 1949. In the early 20th century, Marysvale, Utah was primarily a small farming community.

Lane and Etta Bertelsen were a married couple who lived in this small town. Etta gave birth to the first child born within this marriage, a daughter, on December 11, 1919. The Bertelsens named the newcomer Emily Marie; the world would eventually come to know her as Marie Windsor. Dark-haired and blue-eyed, intelligent and outgoing, Emily Marie Bertelsen showed rich promise early in life. She was intelligent and performed well academically in all subjects save math, a subject she disliked. (Of course, this is all-too-common as many people, including highly intelligent people, are math-anxious and/or math-challenged).

During most of her elementary school years, Emily Marie was an only child. She was eleven years old when Etta delivered her first sibling, her brother Jerry. When she was 17 years of age and a freshman in college, sister Louise was born.

Popular with her peers, the child easily made friends. However, years later she was to recall being disturbed by the way she saw animals treated in Marysvale. "For instance, it was very rare for anyone there with dogs to allow them into the house," the adult Marie Windsor informed a writer. "Often these 'pets' had to sleep outdoors in sub-zero weather even while their owners expected the animals to be their 'best friends.' Sometimes those dogs had to eat snow just to get moisture." She also said, "The way animals were and are abused appalls me to this very day."

Living in a rural area meant she was around horses and learned to ride them when she was but a wee lass. She later said she was given her first horse, Silver Queen, when only about six years old. "At the time we couldn't afford a saddle, so I learned to ride bareback," she recalled. She became quite skilled at horse riding—an aptitude that would sometimes come in handy in her adult career as an actress.

Emily Marie showed musical and dramatic talent from an early age. As a child, she showed an enthusiastic interest in a then-new art form—the motion picture. Her family cheerfully cultivated this interest and her maternal grandmother, whom Emily Marie called "Gunga," often took the child to theaters to see silent movies. The child was enthralled by these early films. Other audience members frequently gave a wide berth to little Emily Marie and Gunga because of the adult woman's habit of reading the subtitles out loud as the film played. Like so many others in the time period, Emily Marie became a fan of Clara Bow. At Emily Marie's young age, she could not understand that Clara Bow's nickname, "The It Girl," meant sex appeal but she could certainly see how eye-catching that star's pretty face and boyish figure were. She could also appreciate the vibrant and dynamic way Clara Bow made characters come to life onscreen.

Perhaps inspired by the movies she saw, Emily also loved playacting on her family's home porch, sometimes with other children, and sometimes by herself, in improvised skits. She knew early on that she was destined for an entertainment career. "I decided when I was eight years old that I wanted to be an actress," she later recalled. Although there were no performers in her family, they "did everything to encourage and help" her pursue her goal. Indeed, her parents recognized that they could be raising a performer and sought to refine her talents into skills. When the child was eleven years old, her parents began driving her 30 miles away, to Richfield, Utah, for weekly lessons in dancing and drama. Happy with the career she had, she once said, "I really wanted to be Clara Bow but that didn't quite work out." She was wonderful at being the actress she was.

Always tall, Marie was also quite athletic and enthusiastically participated in a variety of sports. She was the captain of the girls' basketball team at her junior high school.

Visual arts like drawing also intrigued young Emily Marie.The high school that teenaged Emily Marie attended had no art teacher but the school's principal saw some of the teenager's artistic creations and was strongly impressed. According to information about her in the "Marie Windsor" section of *Utah's Piute County* website," the principal "gave her two books on art and told her if she learned to draw and paint well, he'd give her scholastic credit for her work." That special credit, coupled with the good grades she earned in the standard subjects, meant that she was awarded her high school diploma in only three years rather than the usual four.

At the high school graduation ceremony, school officials at the school honored Emily Marie, and showcased some of her talents, by allowing her to give a special "musical recitation."

After high school, the high-achiever attended Brigham Young University (BYU). At the same time that she studied at BYU, she took classes in drama and dance at the Provo Conservatory. During this time, she performed as the lead in a one-act play entitled *Flood Control.* In a musical called *Flying Along* she performed as a dancer.

Marie also worked at regular jobs while still residing in Utah. For example, she was a telephone operator for a period of time.

In *Killer Tomatoes*, a book about famous film noir actresses, co-author Laura Wagner reports, "After two years she, along with her family, traveled to New York where she wanted to study acting with the famed coach Maria Ouspenskaya; she was frustrated to find that Mme. Ouspenskaya had moved to Hollywood."

When the family returned to Marysvale, Emily Marie won special titles that would open doors for the talented aspiring performer. The pioneer days have long been a popularly cherished part of the history of Utah. Annual celebrations of this aspect of the state's early heritage started in 1931 as "Pioneer Days." These celebrations were re-titled Covered Wagon Days in 1935 (the title became Days of '47 in 1943).

It is unlikely Emily Marie had high hopes for victory when she entered this contest in 1939 since there were no less than 81 young ladies competing for the coveted title. Along with one other BYU female student, Marie was selected to represent the town of Provo in the competition. An article published in a Utah newspaper, *The Daily Herald*, described Marie as "the most statuesque of all contestants." It gave a rundown of her activities, reporting that she "dances, skis, swims, golfs, plays tennis and is a horsewoman." It also mentioned her "dramatic training." This brief article was accompanied by photographs of Marie and the other young lady representing Provo. Marie's photograph shows her looking down with a bashful expression, her hair up.

She won the contest. A later article in *The Daily Herald* stated, "A popular Brigham Young University brunette co-ed from Marysvale, Utah, today was prepared to reign as queen of Salt Lake City's 1939 Covered Wagon Days celebration."

In 1940, the Marysvale Chamber of Commerce unofficially bestowed the title of "Miss Utah" on Emily Marie Bertelsen. This allowed her to enter a Gateway to Hollywood contest—which took her straight to that fabled entertainment capital. Fruits of this victory included a $100 prize. She also contacted renowned drama teacher Maria Ouspenskaya who agreed to accept her as a pupil. Etta and Lane drove their daughter to Hollywood in 1940.

A Fledgling Actress Stretches Her Wings

2

THE ELDER BERTELSENS RETURNED HOME, leaving their daughter to stay with friends of the family before moving into the Hollywood Studio Club. One of Emily Marie's friends at the Club was actress Carole Matthews with whom she would one day work in the 1956 film *Swamp Women*. The place also served as home to such up-and-coming luminaries as Marilyn Monroe, Donna Reed, and Ruth Roman. It was during this Hollywood Studio Club period that Emily Marie rechristened herself with the name "Marie Windsor" by which she would always be known. She was six months into a nine-month course with Maria Ouspenskaya when Marie's parents sent word that they did not have the money to continue the classes. Marie found ways to earn money so she could pay for them herself. She got jobs both inside and outside the entertainment industry. She worked as a telephone operator and "cigarette girl" in the well-known Mocambo Hollywood nightclub; she also did fashion modeling, radio work, and appeared onstage. She worked in a store, first as a salesperson and then as a model.

Under the tutelage of Maria Ouspenskaya, the fledgling actress made her California theater debut in a play called *Forty Thousand Smiths* that opened in October 1940 at the Ben Bard theater in Hollywood. She was the female lead in the play. It was also in this theater production that she first appeared under the name by which the world would know her: Marie Windsor. Perhaps, as often happens, she just liked her middle name better than her first. Why choose Windsor as a surname? A friend who enjoyed following the doings of European royals suggested she adopt the name of the family that reigns—although hardly rules—in the United Kingdom.

Marie enjoyed learning from Maria Ouspenskaya. Marie also seemed impressed by her style in wearing "silver Indian rings and bracelets." The budding actress noted that the bracelets Ouspenskaya sported "jingled all the time, especially when she was giving me a critique." What sort of critique? "She seemed to like me very much but was always working on me to deliver more 'inner energy,'" Marie remembered.

The young woman re-christened as Marie Windsor made the acquaintance of producer LeRoy Prinz. He saw that she had a future in show business and helped her get a Screen Actors Guild (SAG) card. This enabled her to get film work, albeit usually uncredited extra parts.

Continuing work at the Mocambo, she found it difficult. An article in *The Herald* of Provo, Utah noted that Marie's boss was an alcoholic and a "verbally abusive" woman. She was also not earning enough to comfortably support herself. "I was very upset because the people who ran the concessions wouldn't let us keep the tips," she later told interviewer Skip E. Lowe. "They'd split with us if it were over $5." Producer Arthur Hornblow found young Marie weeping over the cigarettes she was selling. "You really want to be an actress?" he rhetorically asked. "You don't really want to be a cigarette girl?" She easily acknowledged the truth of those observations. He promised to help get her more work in her chosen field. He made an appointment with a dance director who hired her to work as an extra on the 1941 Hal Roach musical entitled *All-American Co-Ed* starring John Hall and Frances Langford. In this film, Marie appeared as a "Carrot Queen"—how's that for kitsch? *All-American Co-Ed* was pivotal to Marie's career in a practical way. "That's how I got my guild card," Marie recalled.

After appearing in *All-American Co*-Ed, Marie strolled on a sidewalk in *Unexpected Uncle*, patronized an inn in *Weekend for Three*, sat in a nightclub in *Playmates* (all three of which movies were released in 1941). She may have been little more than decoration in *Playmates* but it is likely the movie had a special place in Marie's heart as she appeared with John Barrymore. What's more, the legendary John Barrymore autographed a photograph of himself for the budding actress!

Marie was a Frenchwoman in a café in *Joan of Paris*, a young lady applying her makeup in *Four Jacks and a Jill*, a pretty woman on a tour in *Call Out The Marines*, a princess in *The Lady or the Tiger?*, a "native" in *Flying with Music*, and a member of "Company C" in *Parachute Nurse*, all motion pictures that first graced the screen in 1942. During this period, she got to know some who were already famous. "I used to go to Clark Gable's ranch to ride," she said.

While taking on film extra work, Marie was still busy as a voice actress heard over the radio waves. She also caught the eye of some well-known entertainers with whom she enjoyed dates. In August 1941, an issue of *Radio Guide* reported, "Rudy Vallee out with a good-looker, name, Marie Windsor."

During this period, Marie plied her craft on the stage on occasion. In a play called *Stardust* that journalist Mark A. Miller described as a "flop," Marie worked as an understudy for Gloria Grahame. "Gloria and I became friends," Marie stated. "I liked her and she always seemed a little nicely off-the-wall to me." Marie did not spend all her time in Hollywood but sometimes returned to New York City where she played a villainess in the Broadway hit *Follow the Girls*.

MGM executives were impressed by Marie's work and offered her a two-year contract which she signed. "Although her parts were small, the studio enrolled her in a highly beneficial, vigorous acting, singing, and dancing curriculum."

She had extra roles in several 1942 flicks including *Joan of Paris* in which she warmed a seat in a café, *Four Jacks and a Jill* in which she is seen applying make-up, and *The Big Street* in which she was a nightclub patron. She may not have been able to show off much acting talent in those tiny roles but it is a certainty that she beautified the atmosphere!

Marie Meets *Smart Alecks*

1942 ALSO SAW HER get her first screen credit—hooray! hooray!—as a nurse in the "East Side Kids" comedy *Smart Alecks*.

The East Side Kids followed the Dead End Kids and the Little Tough Guys and preceded the Bowery Boys. Each of these groups were made up of sometimes changing bands of actors playing rambunctious teenaged street kids in light-hearted and energetic comedies. Leo Gorcey, playing "Muggs" McGinnis, was prominent in the ESK series as a fledgling hoodlum given to clumsy talk as when he observes that "an optimist is one who looks at the good side and a pacifist is one who looks at the bad side" and believes "monetary" is "where they bury people" and complains that distractions are "interrupting my conservation." The motion pictures in the ESK series were hampered by low budgets and predictable storylines but they remain popular to this day because of their energy, sprightly pace, and the way the members of the gang are depicted as kind-hearted and caring beneath their rowdy exteriors. As is all-too-common in films about teenagers, the actors playing the delinquent juveniles are usually quite obviously of voting age—even back when an American got the franchise at age twenty-one. The gang was all-white except for one African-American member, Scruno, who is listed in the credits as "Sunshine Sammy" rather than by the actor's actual name, Ernest Morrison.

Marie Windsor is listed last in the *Smart Alecks* screen credits as "Nurse." Her role was a bit part but Windsor had to be delighted that she saw her name on celluloid.

A poster advertising *Smart Alecks* proclaimed, "Those roughneck rascals are running wild again!" In a frank appeal to the sensational, it promises, "Compared to the East Siders, a gorilla is a household pet!"

The plot to a large extent revolves around the yearning of the ESK gang for baseball uniforms. They are startled to find one gang member, Hank, decked out in fancy clothes and possessing an unusual amount of cash. They learn that the "Kid" is working for grown-up bad guys like Butch Blake (Maxie Rosenbloom). ESK leader Muggs is unwilling to accept the "dirty money" that Hank has been making with the true tough guys and expels him from the gang. Hank learns just how foolish he was to play with the big boys when he is arrested for being a lookout during a bank robbery. The robbers escape detection but Hank is put behind bars when he refuses to rat on his crime bosses. The sister of an ESK named Danny, Ruth Stevens, reluctantly testifies against Hank. Despite having kicked him out of the ESK clubhouse, his old pals still have affection for him and are mad at her for cooperating with the cops. In an odd twist, gangster Blake makes off with an ESK baseball and is grabbed by Danny. Then Danny and everyone else learns that Blake is actually gangster Butch Broccoli. A series of machinations follow that lead to Danny being badly beaten, hospitalized, and at death's door.

A review of *Smart Alecks* that appeared in the *Los Angeles* times on June 22, 1942 began, "Delving just a little deeper into life's realities but yet keeping a refreshing humor, those good bad boys, the East Side Kids, live up to their reputation for okeh acting in their latest chapter, 'Smart Alecks.'" The reviewer, identified only as "G.K.," notes that Leo Gorcey branches out from his usual comedy into drama in some serious scenes in which he "reveals much ability."

Indeed, *Smart Alecks* is an odd mishmash of genres, mixing realistic comedy with cartoonish comedy as when an ESK "swallows" a harmonica and Muggs extracts it through "some chiropracty" or a character is fed cake frosting made of soap and does not even notice. It also has elements of crime drama and even genuine pathos as G.K. noted in the contemporary review just quoted.

Marie Windsor's unnamed nurse only appears in a couple of scenes toward the end of the film, one of them the very last scene. In both, she tolerantly allows "East Side Kids" to flirt. In the first, she walks down the corridor when Glimpy (Huntz Hall) flirtatiously asks if she might operate on him, suggesting she might "cut my heart out." She gently suggests his heart might still belong to Mama. The film ends with Gorcey kissing her—and then pours water over his own head to cool off the passions that kiss aroused! Although it was not a major or demanding part, the film sweetly pays tribute to pretty Marie Windsor's power over heterosexual manhood. It also held the distinction of being Gorcey's very first onscreen kiss! There surely were many men who would have envied him for being kissed by lovely Marie Windsor.

Many years later, Marie said she believed she only worked two days to make the two scenes in which she appeared in *Smart Alecks*. What did she think of the actors who made up the "East Side Kids"? "The boys were all nice kids, although a couple of them seemed to be a little less 'fun-nutty' than the others," she said. "I seemed to favor Stanley Clements and Leo Gorcey because they helped put me at ease." She continued that their kindness to her may have been because she was "naïve and green."

4 "M.E. Windsor" and Jack Benny

NEEDLESS TO SAY, extra work did not make enough money for adequate support. Marie Windsor was employed as a salesperson in the lingerie section of a department store—also modeling for the store—when she began writing gags and mailing them to Jack Benny. She sent them to the famous comedian as "M. E. Windsor." The reason for this pen name? "I used my initials because I was afraid he might be prejudiced against a woman gag writer," she revealed. Benny liked the gags so much he asked M. E. Windsor to meet him so they could discuss the prospect that Windsor would work as a staff writer for him at Warner Brothers.

When Benny met "M. E. Windsor," he was startled by her beauty—and probably by her gender. He learned of her acting ambitions, and introduced the budding actress to producer Jerry Wald. From there she signed a contract for a small role as a "dream girl" in Benny's next film, *George Washington Slept Here* (1942). That comedy was based on a play of the same name by George S. Kaufman and Moss Hart. The storyline is that Connie Fuller (Ann Sheridan) and Bill Fuller (Jack Benny) are evicted from their New York City apartment because their dog harmed the carpet. Connie persuades Bill to move to a rural house that has as its claim to fame the story that the Father of Our Country once took a snooze there. Along with its co-stars, the film boasted dependable supporting actors Percy Kilbride and Hattie McDaniel. The light-hearted comedy received generally good reviews. However, it is unlikely to have done much for Marie's career. "There were script changes and my part was written out of the picture," she explained to an interviewer.

Uncredited extra work followed as an Inca Princess in the short film *Inca Gold* (1943), a hostess in *Chatterbox* (1943), and a bystander at a dock in *The Iron Major* (1943).

That busy year of 1943 saw Marie take a break from the silver screen to return to the stage. She joined up with a vaudeville-style troupe known as "Henry Duffy's Merry-Go-Rounders." The show opened in Detroit, traveled to Buffalo, and went on to Washington, D.C. where it closed.

After that closing, Marie traveled to New York City. In the Big Apple, Marie worked on the stage. Additionally, radio producer Jerry Devine hired her as a voice actress. She participated in about 400 radio shows! She did voice work on the radio soap opera *Our Gal Sunday* for nine months.

Marie's strong career orientation did not exclude a private life. She was acting on the program *Amanda of Honeymoon Hill* when she met the man who would became a major romantic interest for her, bandleader and radio actor/host Ted Steele. Hopefully, these two people were smart enough to see the appropriateness of a romance growing out of a meeting on a show with the word "honeymoon" in its title.

On April 21, 1946, the nuptials were held at the Marysvale home of Lane and Etta Bertelsen. After a brief honeymoon, it was back to the stages and radio studios of the Big Apple for Marie and Ted.

Sadly, the Marie Windsor-Ted Steele match did not turn out to be a good one. "He was still in love with his first wife so we rarely lived together," Marie explained. "I soon sought and obtained an annulment and decided to really concentrate on my work."

Marie was cast in a Broadway hit, the musical revue *Follow the Girls*. It had opened in April 1944; Marie was cast as a replacement for a previous cast member several months later. In this revue, Marie worked alongside Jackie Gleason. After Marie played in this show for roughly half a year, an MGM representative asked her to take a screen test for MGM. That test impressed MGM executives. They offered her a short-term contract that she accepted. "was put under a stock contract to MGM for one-and-a-half years, during 1947 and 1948. We had a wonderful group of excellent, renowned coaches on the lot and I was in classes with Elizabeth Taylor, Janet Leigh, Marie McDonald, and many of the people the studio was grooming." Lessons were offered in dancing, voice, diction, and singing.

The contract did not lead to leading roles or even large roles but to more of the sort of extra work and bit parts she had previously done, filling in a film's background as a guest in a nightclub or a cashier behind a counter. Despite the brevity of the appearances she made, author Laura Wagner suggests she brought a special quality to them: "She seemed to indicate in these movies that there was something more waiting to be told, something smoldering just below the surface." She also worked as a "Vargas model." Alberto Vargas was famous for his paintings of "pin-up" women. Marie later recalled, "At MGM, they called a couple of us starlets to pose."

Her extra work, stints in bit parts, kiss in *Smart Alecks*, and Vargas modeling had garnered enough attention that, along with another up-and-coming performer, she was featured in a small piece in *The Los Angeles Times*. Published on November 7, 1946, was a photograph of Marie, actress Mary Stuart, and an unnamed female store cashier. The photograph was captioned "Not Much Time" and reported, "Beating the deadline for Christmas card ordering were starlets Mary Stuart, left, and Marie Windsor, center, who made selections from stocks downtown." This would not be the only time the *Los Angeles Times* reported on an "ordinary" activity of Marie's. On August 23, 1947, the newspaper ran a photograph of Marie and fellow actress Jean Dean (also a Vargas model) with their arms around actor Frank Morgan. They were accompanied by two kilted men playing bagpipes to the side of the trio. The caption called it a "Hollywood Welcome" and noted that Morgan's "yacht won a recent race to Honolulu" and "was greeted aboard liner Matsonia on his return yesterday by Jane Dean and Marie Windsor, while couple of kilted lads serenaded him." ["Lads" does not denote youth in this case as both bagpipe players appear to be middle-aged and one seems to have gray hair.]

5

Song of the Thin Man Swan Song

MARIE WAS CAST in a small but credited—and important—part in the 1947 *Song of the Thin Man*. The "Thin Man" film series (and later TV show) was based on a 1934 novel by Dashiell Hammett entitled *The Thin Man*. That book introduced the world to a dynamic, witty, and very loving married couple named Nick and Nora Charles. The happy couple solved crimes together. In their continuing affection and attraction for each other, Nick and Nora Charles were a kind of modern advertisement for the ancient institution of marriage. To a large extent, what made them so fascinating was not just the interest Nick and Nora held as individual characters but the interest their marriage created.

There is an irony in the creation of these entrancing characters and their vibrant marriage. Hammett modeled the couple on himself and his longtime girlfriend, playwright Lillian Hellman. While the intimacy and cooperation as well the affectionate repartee of the Charleses acts as a kind of advertisement for the institution of marriage, the couple on whom they were modeled never wed! Of course, that irony hardly detracts from the entertainment value of Nick and Nora Charles.

Dashiell Hammett's successful novel led to the making of *The Thin Man* as a motion picture in 1934, the same year in which the book was released, that starred William Powell and Myrna Loy in the roles of Nick and Nora Charles. The success of that movie led to a series of five sequels: *After the Thin Man* (1936), *Another Thin Man* (1939), *Shadow of the Thin Man* (1941), *The Thin Man Goes Home* (1945), and the final 1947 *Song of the Thin Man* in which Marie appeared in the role of Helen Amboy, wife of a big-time criminal.

Marie enjoyed the company of stars Loy and Powell. She had previously met Myrna Loy at small dinner parties. "Myrna was a friendly and good-natured woman and Bill Powell was an adorable, witty, and most classy gentleman," she fondly recalled.

I have already mentioned the irony that the marriage of Nick and Nora constitutes a kind of praise of marriage itself but was modeled on an unmarried couple. There is a further irony in the title of the "Thin Man" series that goes back to the novel itself. In that book, the "thin" character is the victim. However, the title became so associated with the series that people thought of Nick Charles as "The Thin Man" which is why the series always had the term in each of its titles.

Directed by Edward Buzzell with a screenplay by Steve Fisher and Nat Perrin, the movie begins on a gambling ship, the *S. S. Fortune.* Ladies and gentlemen in the upper-class garments characteristic of the 1940s are eagerly gathered around roulette wheels and slot machines. The owner of the *Fortune*—and a man who clearly possesses a fortune—is Phil Brant (Bruce Cowling). A charity benefit is taking place this evening with the entertainment for this benefit from a jazz band led by Tommy Drake (Phillip Reed). Prominent musicians in the band are Fran Page (Gloria Grahame) and clarinet player Buddy Hollis (Don Taylor).

At the benefit, the lovely blonde Fran skillfully sings *You're Not So Easy To Forget.* (Actress Gloria Grahame is not singing but lip synching as she usually did when a character she played had to warble a tune. Grahame was a truly gifted actress, who contributed greatly to motion pictures, but she was notoriously unable to carry a tune.)

At one point, Hollis takes center stage with his clarinet. The music is first-rate but the clarinetist's hair is disheveled and he has an "off" facial expression that will later be revealed as the result of mental instability.

Soon after regaling the benefit attendees with some lively 1940s jazz, bandleader Drake goes to Brant to inform the latter that Brant will soon lose a bandleader. Drake will lead elsewhere as agent Mitchell Talbin (Leon Ames) has wrangled a better booking.

However, Drake has a problem: he is up to his eyeballs in debt, owing gangster Al Amboy (William Bishop) no less than a whopping $12,000 (of even much more value in those days, when that amount was more than the average American family's yearly income). When the gangsters learns that Drake plans to take his services elsewhere, he demands Drake cough up the debt in total that very night. The pressed upon Drake begs Talbin for an advance in the amount of… you guessed it. Talbin is understandably unwilling to advance $12,000.

By now, Drake has become panicky in his desperation to repay the gangster. Knowing that Brant has a safe in his office, Drake sneaks into it and opens the safe. But he is shot from behind by someone neither he nor the audience sees.

In a parallel plot development, Brant elopes with socialite Janet Thayar (Jayne Meadows). They do not have a "regular" wedding because Thayer's snooty high-society father, David Thayer (Ralph Morgan), looks down on Brant. Although Brant is "in the money," the elder Thayer is offended by his wrong-side-of-the-tracks background. The morning after the couple wed, they visit the apartment of Nick and Nora Charles. The Brants inform the Charleses that newspaper stories reporting the Brant couple as the last people to see Drake alive are false—and could Nick and Nora help the Brants clear their names?

A shot rings out and Phil Brant just barely manages to avoid a gunshot wound.

The cops are soon at the Charles residence—and Phil Brant is soon in police custody.

Accompanied by the Charles dog, Asta, Nick Charles goes aboard the *Fortune* to search for clues both physically and by talking to witnesses. As in any good mystery, varied twists and turns follow before the malefactor is eventually unmasked.

Marie's role as Helen Amboy, wife to gangster Al Amboy, is quite small. As was true with *Smart Alecks*, her name appeared last in the opening credits. Although the part was essentially a bit, it turned out to be pivotal to the ultimate revelation of the malefactor. Marie glides onto the stage in a flattering evening gown and with an air of confident, even vibrant, sophistication. *Utah's Piute County* quotes an unnamed source as describing the character simply as "a real bitch" and noting that she has a "very good scene in a nightclub."

Song of the Thin Man was the last of the film series—and often regarded as the least well-made. Myrna Loy said she "hated" the movie and derided it as "a lackluster finish to a great series." Although not one of the better *Thin Man* films, *Song of the Thin Man* was entertaining.

There were more films in which Marie did uncredited extra work.

The *Force of Evil*
Big Break

6

MARIE'S BIG BREAK came with the extraordinary 1948 crime drama entitled *Force of Evil*. Abraham Polonsky directed the film and co-wrote the screenplay with Ira Wolfert. It was based on Wolfert's 1943 novel *Tucker's People*. Marie is third billed in the credits.

In *Force of Evil*, John Garfield plays attorney Joe Morse who works for big shot gangster Ben Tucker (Roy Roberts). Tucker is a paragon of ruthless greed. He is also determined to consolidate New York City's numbers racket under his control. Joe is willing to aid Tucker but has a conflict of interest because his older brother Leo Morse (Thomas Gomez) owns a small-fry numbers racket that could be crushed by Tucker's plan.

A clever fellow who is willing to cut moral corners, Joe originates a scheme to help Tucker. Joe bases his scheme on the recognition that, since the United States declared its independence in the year 1776, many people select the last three digits of that year, 776, in Independence Day lotteries. By fixing 776 as the Fourth of July winning number, Joe suggests to Roy, the gangster can bankrupt other numbers banks.

The ins and outs of the story lead to a conflict between Joe and Leo that is Biblical in its dimensions—which the script underlines with references to Cain and Abel—since, as the synopsis on the Turner Classic Movies website observes, Leo "is an intrinsically honest man in a dishonest business" who wants nothing to do with Joe's dirty plan.

There are several interesting characters in the story including Leo's "nice" secretary Doris Lowry (Beatrice Pearson), crusading city prosecutor Link Hall (Arthur O'Connell), timid bookkeeper Freddy Baur (Howard Chamberlain), and Tucker's rival, gangster Bill Ficco (Paul Fix).

Perhaps no "minor" character is more memorable than that of Tucker's wife, Edna Tucker, whom Marie plays. Appearing in only three scenes, Marie oozes a restrained sensuality fused with a classy air of authority. In her first, very brief appearance, Joe is at the Tucker mansion. He is on the telephone as Edna noiselessly enters. She wryly tells Joe, "Sometimes you act like a human being." The audience soon realizes the Tucker marriage is troubled when Marie refers to her husband as "stone" and says he makes her "feel unnecessary."

In her second scene, Joe returns to his office to find the glamorous Mrs. Tucker seated in his chair. She rises to let him have his seat and informs him that she wanted to telephone him. "Telephone me about what?" he inquires. "Telephone you about the telephone," she answers. She lets him know that prosecutor Hall has tapped her husband's telephone and speculates, "You might spend the rest of your life trying to remember what you *shouldn't* have said."

Her final scene shows her running down a hall to open the door for Joe. She has little to do in this scene but her presence reminds the audience of the vulnerability—as well as lust—she aroused in him in her second scene.

Force of Evil is a classic, considered a great film by many critics. It is also a most unusual motion picture. As John Garfield biographer Larry Swindell observes, the movie "smacked of traditional Hollywood in no way." Swindell continues that Polansky as the director "created a powerful, distinctly American film, although not a pretty one by any means."

The trailer for *Force of Evil* frankly referenced a 1947 movie that starred Garfield entitled *Body and Soul*. The director of *Force of* Evil, Abraham Polonsky, supplied the screenplay for *Body and Soul* that was directed by Robert Rossen. A drama that evokes *Faust*, this film is about a young boxer named Charley Davis, played by Garfield. Charley Davis is drawn into the web spun by an unscrupulous promoter named Roberts (Lloyd Gough). The young boxer faces a series of increasingly nasty ethical dilemmas.

Born in 1913 to Jewish immigrants from Russia, John Garfield carved out a distinctive screen persona as an alienated, often impoverished, hero or anti-hero. He is believed by many critics to have prefigured the sort of non-conformist masculine figures often played by such later actors as Marlon Brando, James Dean, Dennis Hopper, and Dustin Hoffman. Along with *Body and Soul* and *Force of Evil*, he is famous for his portrayal of drifter turned murderer Frank Chambers opposite Lana Turner in *The Postman Always Rings Twice*.

A political liberal, Garfield is often considered a victim of the infamous Red Scare in the 1950s. In April 1951, he appeared before the House Un-American Activities Committee (HUAC). He told the Committee that he was not a Communist and had never been one. However, he declined to "name names" of people he knew who might actually have been Communists. About a year later, on May 20, 1952, playwright Clifford Odets testified before HUAC. During that testimony, Odets was asked if he knew anything about John Garfield being a Communist and Odets said he was certain Garfield had never been a Communist. The next day, on May 21, 1952, John Garfield suffered a fatal heart attack. He was only 39 years old when he died. His funeral was attended by thousands.

Abraham Polonsky also fell to the Red Scare. Blacklisted after *Force of Evil*, he would not direct another film until 1969 when he directed *Tell Them Willie Boy Is Here*. Unlike many others who were blacklisted for communist affiliations, Polonsky actually *was* a Communist Party member. Like others blacklisted, he continued to work in cinema behind fake names and fronts. He also kept his Marxist beliefs until his death in 1999.

There is no question that *Force of Evil* is primarily John Garfield's vehicle but Marie was prominent in it and that was reflected in the film's advertising. The film trailer boasts, "Gang Trouble! Girl Trouble! Garfield!" It soon shows Garfield talking on the phone while lovely Marie, a-glitter with jewelry, places a cigarette in his mouth. A powerful sensuality hovers over the brief interchange.

Force of Evil was a genuine breakthrough for Marie: it was the first motion picture in which she received featured billing as well as the first in which her picture appeared in its print advertisements. In *Killer Tomatoes*, Wagner calls Marie's performance "unforgettable" and continues, "Marie's edgy talents had at last been on display." Wagner writes that, with the part of Edna Tucker, "She finally was given a role to sink her teeth into and from then on would generally attack each part with the same ferocity."

When released, *Force of Evil* got mixed reviews. A *New York Times* review by critic Bosley Crowther called it "a cold, hard, relentless dissection of a bitter, aggressive young man who lets himself get in too deep as the lawyer for a 'policy racket' gang." After pointing out the unpleasantness of the subject and characters, the review praised the movie as "a dynamic crime-and-punishment drama, brilliantly and broadly realized."

Crowther continued, "It gathers suspense and dread, a genuine feeling of the bleakness of crime and a terrible sense of doom. And it catches in eloquent tatters of on-the-wing dialogue moving intimations of the pathos of hopeful lives gone wrong."

Today, *Force of Evil* is widely regarded as brilliant. In a special feature on a Blu-ray edition of the movie, famed director Martin Scorsese reveals that he introduced fellow famed directors Francis Ford Coppola and Michael Powell to the film and also suggested watching it to actor Robert De Niro. Scorsese calls *Force of Evil* "a major influence on my work… particularly on *Mean Streets, Raging Bull,* and *Goodfellas.*" In an essay devoted to *Force of Evil*, David Thomson asserts, "What makes the film so uncommon and so much more than a noir melodrama is the way that controlled tension between criminal lowlifes and poetic talk is matched by the stylization of décor and action soaring above the elements of a crime film."

Special challenges of a very practical and physical character had to be met in *Force of Evil* as well as her next movie. As would so often be the case, the 5'9" Marie stood taller than her leading man. Thus, high heels were definitely out when she did a scene opposite Garfield. The camera operator took care to ensure she did not appear to tower over him.

Force of Evil definitely jump-started Marie Windsor's acting career. The oft-time extra and bit player had shown her acting chops. She was now in demand for major roles.

7 Marie In Major Film Roles

IN MARIE'S NEXT MOTION PICTURE, the 1949 *Outpost in Morocco*, she co-starred with George Raft. Directed by Robert Florey, it tells a story about the French Foreign Legion in Morocco. Raft plays Captain Paul Gerard, a compulsively promiscuous French Legionnaire. His habit of making passes at every female he sees is remarked upon by more than one character early on in the film. His character is said to be irresistible to women so it is not entirely surprising that Marie's Princess Cara, the daughter of a Moroccan Emir, become enchanted by him. The film was hardly inspired but Hagen and Wagner have a point when they assert that Marie's "glacial, exotic beauty (minus accent), her regal bearing and fiery temper elevated the silly, banal story." As the quoted authors noted, Marie did not even attempt an appropriate accent in the film. However, she was a likable figure as she falls completely in love with Raft's French Legionnaire even though she knows theirs will hardly be considered a suitable attachment for the daughter of an emir. The article on Marie in *Utah's Piute County* reports, "Both critics and audiences liked her as the sympathetic Princess Cara."

Making movies in a row with John Garfield and then George Raft meant making movies with two male actors who had something in common that was both interesting and unusual: Marie said Garfield and Raft were the only two male stars who did not mind her being taller than they were. What's more, Raft gave her advice about how to make her height less conspicuous. "Raft told me how to walk with him in a scene," Marie recalled. "We'd start off in a long shot normal, and about the time we got together in a close-up, I'd be bending my knees so I'd be shorter." The dance scene she did with Raft may have been one of the most challenging aspects for her of making *Outpost in Morocco*. "I had to do a tango with Raft and I learned to dance in ballet shoes with my knees bent!" she explained.

Marie later called *Outpost in Morocco* an "exciting movie" but felt it missed something by being filmed in black and white. "The costumes on the set were so colorful," she said, that filming in color would have "enriched" the movie.

Marie very much enjoyed working with Raft: "He was a very sweet, gentle man and very quiet. He was certainly very courteous, nice, and warm to me. He treated me like I was already a movie star. Anything I wanted on the set, I was to have immediately. He was a dear man."

Her casting in roles nasty and foreign reflected a truth about Marie's appearance that would simultaneously help and hinder her career. Marie Windsor was a beauty but hers was not a conventional cookie-cutter type of beauty. Her big eyes and sensuous mouth, as well as her height, meant she was not usually chosen for A-list standard leading lady roles but was considered perfect when a dash of the decadent or unexpected was desired. Laura Wagner wrote in *Killer Tomatoes*: "Her face gave her away: the half-smirk, her shadowy eyes and that *look* were sure signs that she was up to no good, even when she wasn't. You somehow suspected her motives might just be tainted." Wagner continues that this appearance tended to work against her casting in "traditionally romantic leading roles" but was "great viewing for her fans who *wanted* her to be bad, *wanted* her to gun down the next dope who came along." The very unconventionality of her beauty made her suited for playing characters who were "ruthless or just plain tough." However, it was acting talent, not just her looks, that meant she could imbue such roles with "a visceral, raw energy."

The Beautiful Blonde from Bashful Bend (1949) was a Western comedy that starred Betty Grable, Cesar Romero, and Rudy Vallee. Marie had a bit part as a showgirl. Whereas she had played a Moroccan princess with no attempt to accent her English, in this movie she attempted an accent for her role as a French showgirl. But she was none-too-proud of the results, saying she despised her "terrible French accent." However, along with film experience and a paycheck, she gained a lifelong friendship. "We met on that picture," Cesar Romero recalled of his friendship with Marie.

<h1 style="text-align:right">The Fabulous Fable
of Hellfire</h1>

8

1949 ALSO SAW THE RELEASE of *Hellfire*, a Western in which she co-starred opposite William Elliott. *Hellfire* was a product of Republic Pictures Corporation, a production and distribution company that started in 1935 and folded in 1967. An essay about the company by Farran Smith Nehme observed that many movie aficionados know Republic from seeing its logo, a huge eagle atop a mountain, at the start of such classics as *The Quiet Man* (1952) and *Johnny Guitar* (1954). As Nehme notes, it concentrated on Westerns and "all but invented the 'singing cowboy.'" Republic had cost constraints so, while *Hellfire* is a color film, it was filmed not in the rainbow variety of Technicolor but a less expensive in-house color process called Trucolor. Thus, in *Hellfire* "nearly everyone is dressed in some variation of blue, and every part of the landscape seems brown, umber, and orange." The limited palette works to *Hellfire*'s benefit, Nehme observes, because it lends "a dreamy, fable-like quality to this tale."

Hellfire is one of the most unusual Westerns ever made. Directed by R. G. Springsteen and written by Dorrell McGowan and Stuart McGowan, it is aesthetically remarkable and tells an enthralling story that captivates the viewer from its first to last moment. The title of the motion picture conjures damnation but the film has a message of Christian redemption. It also has a powerful feminist message. (It should be acknowledged that some Christians, including Complementarians, Biblical patriarchy advocates, and Christian Domestic Discipline adherents, believe their faith is the polar opposite of gender equality but promotes a male dominant-female submissive ideology; other Christians, often called Egalitarians, see their faith as leading to fewer restrictions based on gender and as opening up all roles to qualified people regardless of genitalia. This is not the place to discuss that theological debate or any other but it is relevant to the messages put forward in *Hellfire* to note that at least *some* Christians believe that what many call a "feminist" message is not only compatible with their faith but intrinsic to it. Other socio-political disputes have occurred in Christianity as it has been used to argue both for and against slavery, racism, anti-semitism capitalism, social welfare measures, and so on).

The actor who stars opposite Marie in *Hellfire* is credited as "William Elliott" but he was usually known as "Wild Bill Elliott," a name he won due to his acting in many Western flicks.

Elliott insisted on Marie Windsor as his co-star. "Bill Elliott saw the test I'd made as well as the George Raft film," Marie remembered. "When he learned I was a horsewoman, he fought the studio to use me instead of one of their contract players." Her facility with horses went back to her small town childhood and had previously been useful in *Outpost in Morocco*; working on *Hellfire* led her to develop another skill that would be useful in future Western movies. "He [Bill Elliott] taught me how to twirl guns," she explained. "I did a lot of stunt work in this Western that normally an actress simply would not do." Marie later said that another actress, Adrian Booth, wanted the part and went to an executive asking for it. "I felt badly because, by rights, the part should have been hers," Marie said. "She was under contract to the studio." After Marie got the part, she sent a dozen roses to Adrian Booth. There was apparently no bitterness between the two performers; decades later, at an event held in 1999, Marie said, "We talked about that."

Hellfire opens with roaring flames. Then we hear and see the message: "Man, with his own misdeed, kindles his own HELLFIRE!" We see shooting and brawling and drinking and a man apparently forcing a kiss on an unwilling woman.

The story proper starts with a preacher in a saloon warning its patrons to turn from their wicked ways. That preacher, Brother Joseph, is played by H. B. Warner. Perhaps significantly, Warner played Jesus Christ in Cecil B. DeMille's 1927 silent movie *The King of Kings*.

The wicked Western town needs a church, Brother Joseph tells the saloon clients. Will someone put a contribution to this noble goal in his hat?

A young fellow contemptuously pours the contents of a shot glass into the preacher's hat. Appearing to come out of nowhere is a fist punching the youth onto the floor. The slugged man sees that this punishment was meted out by renowned gunslinger Zeb Smith (William Elliott). The slugged youth realizes it is in his best interest to hurry out of the place.

"Thank you, friend, but you shouldn't have done that for me," a grateful Brother Joseph tells Zeb.

"For you?" Zeb incredulously replies. "That was my drink he took!"

It is soon revealed that Zeb is a card cheat. His shady ways are disclosed when fellow card players spot the card literally hidden in a sleeve. In the ensuing confrontation, Brother Joseph takes a bullet meant for Zeb.

Having his life saved by the devout Christian leads to a kind of "crisis of non-faith" for Zeb. Nasty as he has been, he feels obligated to repay the minister for saving his life. Brother Joseph tells Zeb to make it right by raising the funds to get that church built. The preacher adds that, when gathering the money for the church, Zeb must follow what the preacher calls "the rule book" that he hands to Zeb—the Bible.

Our former hearty sinner sets out to raise money for that church. The film is realistic in showing that even though Zeb thinks of himself as a reformed character, the card cheating and gun slinging man has trouble following Biblical precepts! Indeed, the character is as aware as the audience of the irony of his lapses of temper as when he roughs up a man who spits in his hat rather than put in a few coins for the church.

Since this is a Western, we are not surprised when, along with Zeb, we witness a quick-on-the-draw cowboy shoot a man outside a saloon. But we get a surprise when the removal of a hat reveals that the shooter is not the man we naturally assumed, but a woman dressed in masculine garb. "Mary!" the wounded man shouts just before taking his last breath.

We soon learn that the shooter is known to the public as the feared outlaw Doll Brown although she was born Mary Carson. The man she gunned down was Lew Stoner (Harry Woods). His three outraged brothers vow revenge on her.

Up rides Marshal Bucky McLean (Forrest Tucker) who informs the brothers Stoner that the law has already put a reward of $5,000 on Doll Brown for an express hold-up. Zeb realizes that $5,000 would build a church.

The odds are stacked against this outlaw as she is being sought by the long arm of the law, the trio whose brother she killed, and our fundraising hero.

Doll Brown has some advantages on her side as she is an expert horse rider and crack shot. We eventually learn that, although she appears tough-as-nails, this outlaw is not the heartless psychopath we first assume. The outlaw who is being sought is herself searching for her long-lost sister Jane Carson.

Zeb seeks to ride with Doll and make friends with her. "I ride alone," the loner declares. But she allows Zeb to ride with her after losing a (rigged?) card game to him. She is quite astounded to learn he plans to build that church with her reward money—and even more astounded that he believes he can use the Bible to persuade her to give herself up.

Various plot twists and turns follow and we learn that Doll lost contact with the younger sister who is so very dear to her because Doll, as Mary Carson, took up with a fellow who did not want her younger sister underfoot. This creep put the sister "on a wagon train going west," causing the loving sisters to lose contact with one another. The villain who did this was Lew Stoner, who fell to the vengeful Doll's bullets.

Since Doll does not have any knowledge of dear Jane's circumstances, where will Doll look for her sister? Doll says she will search for Jane in "dancehalls and saloons." Zeb wonders why he believes Jane Carson is apt to be in such places.

"This is a man's country," Doll answers. "A girl making a living hasn't got much. I know what I'm talking about because I had to live that way myself until I learned how to use this [she touches her gun]." She recalls how the limited choices available to the female sex necessitate hypocrisy: "Laughing when men pawed you when you really wanted to kick them in the face." Doll intends to use the "express money" so Jane can "live like a lady."

Just as there is more to Doll's banditry than we first realize, it turns out there is more to the Marshal's chasing of Doll Brown than law enforcement dedication. He is married to the former Jane Carson! He wants to kill Doll Brown because he believes his wife will be devastated if she learns her sister is a notorious outlaw.

The Marshal seems close to finding Doll Brown and an anxious Zeb tries to block his way into the house in which she hides. Just then, Marie comes out—in a lovely dress. "I'm Julie Gaye," she announces. Marshal Bucky makes no connection between this soft, feminine creature and the notorious Doll Brown.

Zeb knows the subterfuge but he is just as astonished to see what a change a dress and hairdo make. After Bucky leaves, Zeb marvels, "Doll, you're an amazing woman."

"You never called me a woman before," she observes.

"You never looked like one before," he answers.

A variety of plot machinations follow in this Western and it builds to a climax both emotionally moving and artistically satisfying.

To promote *Hellfire*, Marie, accompanied by co-star William Elliott, traveled to Marie's native state of Utah. It was not Marysvale that they appeared in to promote the movie but the state capital of Salt Lake City. Marie said Elliott "set up an opening publicity tour in Salt Lake City for *Hellfire*." The pair of performers appeared on the stage of that city's Lyric Theater in connection with the opening of *Hellfire*.

Critics at the *Los Angeles Examiner* wrote shortly after the picture's release that it was a "sleeper" and praised its story as "entirely plausible." The critics said Marie Windsor had delivered her "finest performance" to date in the film. A review in the *Los Angeles Times* praised the "vivid" nature of Marie's performance, the "restraint" of Bill Elliott's acting, and went on to compliment H.B. Warner, Forrest Tucker, and the others in the film.

On a blog called "The Horn Section," the reviewer asserts, "A western about an outlaw who gets religion *sounds* like a preachy, tiresome endeavor, but director Springsteen and the McGowans deftly evade the potential pitfalls." He elaborates, "The influence of Christianity is shown to be positive" but "limited." He applauds the co-stars, writing, "This show belongs to Elliott and Windsor." The *Marie Windsor Blogathon* states that the film's "spiritual angle" lifts "the redemption theme found in so many Westerns to a new more literal level." The website continues that the movie is a "religious allegory" that is "quite moving." It also notes that there is a "heavy dose of symbolism" in the repeated use of fire in the film, a symbolism appropriate since fire is so often referenced in the Bible.

Posters advertising the movie underlined the twist of an outlaw being female—and appealed to a titillating element—with the words blazoned: "Woman Wanted!" *Hellfire* was sometimes double-billed with a Western from the same year entitled *Brimstone*. One theater wittily had a ticket taker decked out in a devil costume!

Marie's beauty and skill are a big part of what made *Hellfire* a genuine work of cinematic art. As Nehme writes, "Her blue eyes photograph gorgeously in Trucolor." Throughout this demanding role, Marie fully inhabits her character. The shift from the hard, adult-tomboy ruggedness to sweet sashaying femininity could easily seem forced, even absurd, in a less talented actress but Marie pulled it off in a manner that seemed utterly natural. When a mortally wounded Doll Brown recites "The Shepherd's Psalm," Marie superbly conveys Doll Brown's sense of hope in the midst of physical agony and emotional terror. The actress recognized her achievements in this film which, along with *The Narrow Margin* and *The Killing*—was among her three favorites among all of her movies. She said she especially enjoyed playing Doll Brown/Mary Carson because the role was "rich" and "rangy." Marie asserted, "*Hellfire* had a particularly wonderful script and a fabulous part for a woman, namely me. I got to play a woman disguised as a man in the first part of the film. Then my character turned out to be extremely feminine. On top of that, I really enjoyed a chance to use my ability as a horsewoman." In the years to come, Marie often mentioned *Hellfire* in interviews. "I dearly loved that role," she said.

In 2018, New York City's Museum of Modern Art staged a show entitled "Martin Scorsese Presents Republic Rediscovered: New Restorations From Paramount Pictures." At least two Marie Windsor vehicles were featured, one being *Hellfire* and the other *City That Never Sleeps* (1953).

The spectacularly successful performance Marie Windsor delivered in *Hellfire* led to her being cast in a string of Westerns.

Go West, Marie!

9

THE FIGHTING KENTUCKIAN, also released in 1949, starred the one and only John Wayne and featured Marie in a supporting part. It was the first of three movies Marie would do with the Duke. She cherished her memories of working with the superstar. "Duke was a lot of fun on the set," she remarked. "He liked to kid around. Everyone on the Republic lot was a friend of his—the crew, the actors, the general working people. He always had a lot of stories to tell and he loved practical jokes but all the while he was still a serious professional. When it was time to work, he worked." She later recalled that, at a party she attended with Wayne, he jokingly introduced her as "one of his ex-wives." *The Fighting Kentuckian* was written and directed by George Waggner whom Marie found "a lovely man."

The film was set several decades before what is usually regarded as the time of the "Old West." It was inspired by a little-discussed episode in early 19th century history. After Napoleon Bonaparte's famously crushing defeat at Waterloo, his officers and their families were not wanted in France.

A group of exiled former Napoleonic military officers, together with their families, immigrated to the United States. Since Napoleon had been an ally, of sorts, to America during the War of 1812, the U. S. Congress in 1817 granted four Alabama territory townships to the exiles. They created a community named Demopolis.

The plot of *The Fighting Kentuckian* starts when Fleurette DeMarchand (Vera Ralston) makes a shopping trip to Mobile. There she happens upon Kentucky crack shot John Breen (John Wayne). What woman could resist a coonskin capped and fringe-vested John Wayne? Decked out in delicate finery, the exiled young Frenchwoman is just as irresistible to Breen.

As might be imagined, there are obstacles—not the least of which is that Fleurette's father, General Paul DeMarchand (Hugh Haas), has promised her hand to wealthy big shot Blake Randolph (John Howard).

Determined to "get the girl," Kentuckian John Breen detours his regiment to Demopolis where, naturally enough, other complications are encountered. Among them are a group of four con artists out to hoodwink the good people of Demopolis out of their resources. Marie plays con woman Ann Logan.

Perhaps one of the most interesting aspects of *The Fighting Kentuckian* is Breen's sidekick Willie Paine who is played by none other than Oliver Hardy of (Stan) Laurel and Hardy fame. Stan Laurel was ill so Hardy took a break from their partnership to work without him in this film. The chemistry between Wayne and Hardy was so good that Wayne wanted Hardy to become a regular comic sidekick. However, when Stan Laurel recuperated, Hardy decided the tried-and-true formula was best. "Hardy was a sweet gentleman," Marie recalled. "He chuckled a lot and liked to chitchat on the set."

Another oddity of the flick was the casting of Ralston and Haas as French exiles. Both were Czech immigrants. Apparently the filmmakers believed an eastern European accent would be unfamiliar enough to most Americans to be taken as a French accent.

Marie's Ann Logan is seen singing in the film but it was not her voice heard by the audience. She later said she believed it was Marni Nixon whose voice was dubbed into it. The character of Ann Logan called upon Marie to play a baddie who initially hides her true colors from those around her. As Laura Wagner aptly puts it, Ann Logan comes on "acting the innocent but double-crossing everyone in sight." Wagner elaborates that Ann appears "all sweetness" but is revealed as a "greedy, callous" woman.

The Fighting Kentuckian was not a commercial success but it is an entertaining film and Marie, as usual, shone in her part.

The new decade of the 1950s was also the dawn of television in America's living rooms. Thus, the first year of the new decade 1950, saw Marie make several motion pictures for the big screen—*and* make her debut on the small screen. Her cinema work that was released in 1950 included the Westerns *Dakota Lil*, *The Showdown*, and *Frenchie*. There was an interruption in the Western line in the 1950 *Double Deal*, a contemporary crime drama.

In *Dakota Lil*, Marie starred alongside George Montgomery and Rod Cameron. Theatrical release posters play up Marie's work in the film by showing her in pants and shirt holding pistols in each hand but also displaying a background picture of her and a male star kissing. As would so often be the case in shoot-'em-ups, Marie's Dakota Lil was both flamboyantly androgynous and enticingly feminine. She later recalled that her double was Rod Cameron's sister. The double was limited in what she could do as Dakota Lil, Marie continued, because "she couldn't ride a horse!" As in *The Fighting Kentuckian*, she had scenes in which her character sang and, also as in the other flick, she said Marni Nixon's voice was heard while she lip-synched. However, authors Michael G. Fitzgerald and Boyd Magers wrote in *Ladies of the Western* that "20th Century-Fox records indicate it was Anita Ellis."

Montgomery played secret service agent Tom Horn, a man who earned his chops for successfully tracking down Geronimo. Now—the flick is set in 1899—Horn seeks a group of outlaws colorfully known as The-Hole-in-the-Wall gang. Led by Harve Hogan (Cameron), the desperadoes (who are given to lots of traveling) have done robberies from way up north in Canada to way down south at the border of Mexico. The last big haul was of a shipment of treasury bank notes. Since they were shipped unsigned, they are not valid until the receiving bank's president and cashier sign them. Believing Harve Hogan likely to try to connect with a counterfeiter so he can start using the bank notes, Tom's chief suggests trying to find infamous forger Dakota Lil and enlisting her aid in recovering the loot. Wanting to be incommunicado, Tom is using the alias Steve Garrett when he befriends Dakota Lil who is singing in a cantina in Matamoros, Mexico. A series of plot machinations follow that lead Tom and Lil back to the United States. Lil betrays Tom before realizing at a point in the story that she is in love with him.

Overall, the motion picture was a pretty routine "oater" except for… that except for being Marie who often lent spice to otherwise undistinguished Westerns specifically through the combination of androgyny and femininity previously noted. A "Thumbnail Review" in the *Mirror News* of Los Angeles, California opined, "Best thing this western offers is sultry Marie Windsor." A considerably lengthier review by Wanda Hale in New York City's *Daily News* stated, "Nothing much happens outside of the two men [Harve Hogan and Tom Horn] glaring at each other and Dakota Lil playing first one then the other, until it is established that the lady will gladly give up her career of crime, pay her debt to society, provided it isn't too dear, all for the love of the man who is double-crossing her. And as expected, he falls in love with her and they make a bargain but not before he takes care of the 'Hole in the Wall' outfit." Hale concludes the film is "pretty ordinary." A reviewer for the *Ames Daily Tribune* of Ames, Iowa was a bit more positive, calling *Dakota Lil*, along with the film double-billed with it at local theaters, *Boy From Indiana*, a "pair of swell outdoor 'vacation' movies" that satisfy the "adventure and romance urge." Highlighting Marie's role as the title character, the critic called it "the gun smoke and glory story of a 'she-devil' who sets the Badlands aflame." The reviewer praised it as "an action-packed western, photographed in outdoor color" and "saga of a colorful era in western annals." A reviewer from across America's northern border, in Montreal, Canada, wrote in *The Gazette* that, "If you can accept the Hollywood concept of a never-never land which is a blend of 19th and 20th century costumes and manners, then *Dakota Lil* is a very good sample to see. It has the merit of being paced with speed, full of action with some climaxes that pack plenty of punch." The writer continued, "*Dakota Lil* is effectively filmed in color" and notes that Montgomery does well as the agent "whose heart is captured by Lil who, of course, reforms in time for the close." The review ends with a special tribute to Marie: "Miss Windsor is quite spectacular in the title role." *Variety* called the film "a good western" and observed that Montgomery's desire to find Marie was "nifty" in "more ways than one."

A brief mention in the Glen Falls, New York newspaper *The Post-Star* aptly described *The Showdown* as "a rough-and-ready story of revenge riding the trail herd." The screenplay and the directing were both done by a team: Dorrell McGowan and Stuart E. McGowan. This black and white Western reunited Marie with her *Hellfire* co-star Bill Elliott who plays ex-law officer Shadrach Jones whose brother has been killed. Knowing his brother was a crack shot, he does not believe the man could have been killed in the sort of dueling that is routine in the Old West (at least as interpreted in fiction). Thus, he digs up his brother's corpse. Sure enough, he finds that his brother was shot in the back, making his death a murder.

Shadrach Jones sets out to find his brother's murderer and exact revenge. His investigation leads to him to believe that the murderer is a member of the "Circle K Ranch" that is soon to drive cattle to a Montana reservation. Further research leads him to a hotel where he examines the register book for his brother's name. He finds the name but realizes that someone tried to erase it. In the hotel office, he finds a lovely woman, Marie's character Adelaide Gilbert, relaxing and reading a book. He demands to speak to the hotel's owner and is told he is looking at her. The two have a spat. Jones rips the page with his brother's name on it out of the register. Adelaide pulls a gun and demands it back. After tossing the paper in the fire, Adelaide reveals that the gun does not work and she often uses it as a paperweight.

In another scene, Jones shoots and kills Circle K Ranch's foreman, "Big Mart" Stores (Leif Erickson), after the latter pulls a gun on Jones. Then Jones reveals that he knows Stores was wanted for murder.

The loss of Stores was a significant one for Cap MacKellar (Walter Brennan) as he needed the fellow to lead a cattle drive. Since Jones is familiar with the area that the cattle are supposed to go through, Cap asks Jones to replace the dead fellow as ranch foreman and lead the cattle drive. As he leads the cattle drive, he finds that the business is co-owned by Adelaide Gilbert who is riding along with the drive. Once again, Marie plays a woman in a "man's world." As is usually true of such roles—at least when Marie was the actress cast—her skills are as competent as those of her male counterparts. At the same time, she puts a special spin into the proceedings as a woman. Indeed, in this film, she lacks the androgyny she sometimes affected in *Hellfire* but is always just as feminine as she is lovely. Her femininity is underlined when we get a glimpse of a shapely leg and when she sprays perfume on herself before allowing Jones into her tent.

The Showdown is an entertaining Western with a fair number of twists and turns as well as a lineup of appropriately colorful characters like the one-handed Chokecherry (Rhys Williams) who uses a hook and Mike Shattay (William Ching) who harbors a secret, the disclosure of which is both surprising and emotionally moving. There are also a couple of characters who might not sit well in today's political atmosphere such as "Indian Joe" (Charles Stevens) and Gonzales (Nacho Galindo) who could be seen as stereotypical. The movie keeps the viewer interested, partly because it handles its overall revenge theme well and partly because the storyline gives us several genuine surprises with the strongest one being the eventual revelation of the identity of the murderer. Marie said that, in contrast to many films she made, in *The Showdown*, "I didn't go outdoors—all my scenes were shot on the set."

The 1950 Western *Frenchie* was shot in Technicolor, the perfect way to show off the colorful costumes worn, especially by the female characters, and the beauty of the landscape. Loosely based on the 1939 motion picture *Destry Rides Again*, *Frenchie* was directed by Louis King and its script written by Oscar Brodney. The title character is blonde beauty Frenchie Fontaine, played in a sprightly and sexy manner by Shelley Winters. Frenchie got off to a rough start in life when her father, Frank Dawson, was murdered in a town called Bottleneck when she was only a child. She knows two men were in on the murder and that one was former crime partner Pete Lambert (Paul Kelly)

The orphaned girl was taken in by a family of French ancestry, thus her name. Fifteen years later, Frenchie possesses the sort of streetwise (dusty road wise?) skills often enjoyed by those educated in the School of Hard Knocks. She makes a small fortune in the gambling business in New Orleans where she becomes close friends with a "Countess" played by Elsa Lanchester. We know, of course, that the character is not any kind of actual aristocrat but has bestowed the hoity-toity term on herself.

Together with the Countess, Frenchie returns to Bottleneck, hoping to get even with Pete Lambert. There is a casino in Bottleneck called the Scarlet Angel but when Frenchie visits the establishment, she finds it oddly bereft of clientele. She learned that Bottleneck Sheriff Tom Banning (Joel McCrea) has pretty much "cleaned up" Bottleneck, sending those wanting not-so-clean fun to the nearby town of Chuckaluck. And who should be the big wheel in Chuckaluck? None other than Pete Lambert. However, she does not immediately try to get revenge as she wants to learn the identity of the other man who was in on her father's murder.

Until she can exact revenge, her major goal is to earn money by reviving the Scarlet Angel. Frenchie sends word to a fellow she worked with in New Orleans, Lance Cole (John Russell), requesting his assistance. Lance takes a stagecoach to Bottleneck. Lambert learns of Frenchie's plan so he hatches one of his own to stop Cole's stagecoach trip but it is squashed by Sheriff Banning.

Frenchie, together with Countess and Cole, turns the Scarlet Angel into a bustling casino that even lures some gamblers away from Chuckaluck.

Cole is enamored of Frenchie and fears that a romantic feeling is growing between Frenchie and the Sheriff.

Someone else has reason to feel jealous. The film is about halfway through before we meet Marie's character, Diane Gorman. When we see her, she and husband Clyde Gorman (John Emery) are coming out of a church service. Thus, we know that Diane is one of the town's respectable "ladies." A conversation between Diane and Clyde lets us know that

Diane and Tom Banning were once an item but Diane broke it off to wed Clyde—who fears she still carries a torch for Tom. Those fears are based in truth. Diane confesses to Tom that she married Clyde for his riches and pines for the man she truly loves. Although Tom's feelings for Diane have not died, he is too solid of a man to consider stealing another man's wife.

Diane goes to the Scarlet Angel. Making use of her "respectable woman" credentials, she suggests Frenchie close the place up for the moral good of the town. Understandably skeptical, Frenchie wants to know if there is another reason Diane wants the casino closed. Diane lets it slip that her husband is a "silent partner" in the Chuckaluck casino that Pete Lambert runs—also suggesting that Clyde Gorman was the man involved in Frenchie's father's murder. The two women exchange harsh words which leads to slaps which leads to a full-on punching, scratching, hair-pulling catfight. Casino bystanders are only too thrilled to watch two beautiful women physically battle it out. Scoffing at the brawl to the Countess, a man says, "And you call yourselves the weaker sex!" The Countess retorts "Who does?" as Frenchie and Diane keep at it until Sheriff Banning brings the fight to a halt.

That catfight was not an easy scene for Shelly Winters and Marie Windsor to make. "There were no doubles," Marie stated. "Shelley Winters and I talked it over and decided to do it ourselves. Everybody was happy we did. The fight scene took a day and a half to shoot. We didn't get punched on the nose—but there were a few accidental scratches!" The scene made a strong impression on contemporary reviewers. Shortly after *Frenchie* was released Fred W. Fox wrote for the *Los Angeles Times* that the two actresses "put on a battle" that qualifies as "one of the best screen duels since William Farnum and Tom Santschi smashed each other in *The Spoilers* long ago." (Fox referred to the 1942 film entitled *The Spoilers*.)

Fox described Shelley Winters in *Frenchie* as "a combination of Mae West and Gorgeous George.) He called Marie "a perfect antagonist for her in feminine wiles and fisticuffs." The reviewer noted that the film "opens with a chase sequence and sudden death" and that throughout the movie "the camera is busy with plenty of action and little meditation on the part of the players."

Although the catfight only lasts a few minutes onscreen, it took 67 minutes over two days to shoot. The two actresses prepared themselves for this demanding scene by going to Universal-International studio projection rooms to watch scenes from previous movies of actresses in physical fights such as Paulette Boddard and Rosalind Russell slugging it out in *The Women* and Marlene Dietrich and Una Merkel similarly misbehaving in *Destry Rides Again*. Writing for the *Tyrone Daily Herald* of Tyrone, Pennsylvania, James Padgitt reported, "Director Louis King at first wanted to use doubles in the big scene and get closeups of Marie and Shelley rolling around on the floor." That did not sit well with the actresses who watched the doubles going at it and decided they wanted to do their own stunt work. Both suffered injuries. Winters got cuts and bruises on legs and shoulders; Marie got a badly cut lip.

A reporter for the *Messenger-Inquirer* of Owensboro, Kentucky applauded *Frenchie* for showing "Shelley Winters and Joel McCrea at their colorful western best" and lauding the film for showing an "action-packed story." The journalist continues, "A performance to watch closely is that of Marie Windsor," especially "when she engages Shelley Winters in a barroom brawl that is a spectacular highlight of the film. This writer has witnessed many wildcat femme battles on the screen, but the exciting knockdown-and-drag-out between these two combatants is even greater than the famous mayhem dished out between Marlene Dietrich and Una Merkel in *Destry Rides Again*." Shelley Winters and Marie Windsor had outdone their models.

A *San Francisco Examiner* review praised *Frenchie* as "one of the better Westerns" and lauded Shelley Winters as a "screen spitfire." It also noted the interest of a "good catfight."

Marie had top billing in the 1950 *Double Deal*. A black and white whodunit, it was the first motion picture produced by a recently created business, Bel Air Productions. Another distinction was the its tight shooting schedule. One report said it was filmed in nine days and another in only eight!

Distributed by RKO, *Double Deal* was directed by Abby Berlin. Lee Berman and Charles S. Belden scripted the film from a story by Don McGuire.

Only four minutes over an hour in length, *Double Deal* moves at a fast clip. We see a big bus going down a highway and a sign informing us we are entering Richfield City. Exiting the bus in Richfield is Buzz Doyle (Richard Denning). We will soon learn he is an engineer seeking work and has come to this town due to it being the home of an oil well.

Cut to a bar where lawyer C. D. "Corpus" Mills (Taylor Holmes) is drunk and intent on getting drunker. The bartender, Mike (Jim Hayward), suggests Corpus might wish to head home but the booze-loving gent asserts, "Home is where the heart lies," making the bar a kind of home (perhaps he speaks for a multitude of boozers here).

Buzz finds his way to the bar in search of a meal. It just so happens there is a bowl filled with hardboiled eggs on the bar itself. He is on a barstool, getting the shell off an egg, when Marie's character, Terry Miller, comes out of a backroom to request drinks for the fellows there. Buzz is immediately attracted to her, giving her the once-over, and she tartly states, "There's a burlesque in the next town, mister." Buzz learns that one of the gamblers is an "oil man" so he wants to get to know him. Buzz participates in a card game with Walter Karnes (James Griffith) and Reno Sebastian (Carleton Young), both of whom will play major roles in the story. We learn that Reno possesses an oil well and a ranch. Even though Terry works for Walter, she suggests Walter has used loaded dice. Reno becomes angry but Terry takes a conciliatory tone to smooth things over and avoid possible violence. We learn that Walter has been trying for some time to get hold of Reno's holdings.

Possibly struck by conscience, Terry quits working for the crooked Walter Karnes. A good friend of Reno's, she helps Buzz get work with Reno. It so happens that Reno is in a running feud with his pretty blonde sister Lilli Sebastian (Fay Baker). The two are on bad terms because Daddy's will gave Lilli three wells and Reno only one but Lilli still wants her brother's oil well for herself. There is an oddity in their father's will: if Reno fails to strike oil within 45 days, possession of the well transfers to sis. So far, Reno has failed to get oil going. Buzz believes he has the knowledge that will lead to "oily" success.

When we meet Lilli, we see that she is a sharply dressed and sophisticated blonde who lives in a spacious dwelling. Walter Karns appears again in our story as he is in love with Lilli. He tells her about Buzz who may be able to get her brother's oil well going and about the role Terry had in putting Buzz to work there. "Terry's getting to be a busy little girl," Lilli sarcastically comments.

Soon after Lilli gets the Buzz info, she tries to woo Buzz from Reno. When she fails, she suggests bad things may happen to him.

A few scenes pass before the murdered corpse of Reno is found in the hotel room in which Buzz is staying. Could this be related to Lilli's prediction? Police suspect Buzz, then clear him.

Buzz wants to head out of town. After all, as he says, "My job died on me." Terry informs him that Reno's will left ranch and well to her: she wants him to continue his work.

To straighten out legal details, Terry and Buzz seek the help of attorney Corpus. The filmmakers added a cute quirkiness to *Double Deal* by giving Corpus a frisky pet monkey. Monkey Pepe on his perch is a lovely addition to the movie.

As might be expected, Terry and Buzz find Corpus a bit under the weather. Boozed up as he usually is, Corpus knows the law and he hands the late Reno's will to Terry who immediately decides to take Buzz on as her partner. Corpus mentions that Lilli might make trouble, especially since "Lilli has friends" in high places. Events follow in quick succession and Corpus suggests a "truce" with Lilli could lead to positive results.

Terry meets with Lilli. It does not go well and Terry storms away. Or does she? Immediately after Terry appears to exit, Lilli sees something that obviously terrifies her. Then she is shot and killed.

Cops take Terry into custody. Lawyer Corpus comes into police office to demand his client be freed. A cop points out that Reno was killed and Terry got his estate. Her gains were threatened by Lilli who was then murdered. How could it be anyone but Terry? Clever Corpus points out that Terry could be the next intended victim. Reno owned part of an estate and was murdered; Lilli owned part and was murdered; now Terry owns it. There is a pattern here, Corpus argues, indicating Terry is more likely a target than a murderer. "Let her go!" he demands. "But watch her—that will bring the killer out into the open."

Terry is allowed to leave. Is Terry, whom Marie has played very sympathetically, really a serial murderer? Or is she hunted by the true murderer? *Double Deal* is a cheaply made flick but it does what a good mystery ought to do and keeps us guessing until the final unmasking. It even, to some extent, makes "monkeys" out of its baddies and releases a "gusher" of goodness for its good characters! (Readers who watch the flick will get the points made.)

The next year, 1951, saw Marie in the Western *Little Big Horn*. Charles Marquis Warren wrote and directed the movie that was based on a story penned by Harold Shumate. According to Marie, finances caused difficulties in making this flick. "Lippert made the movie," she observed. "They announced on the set they were out of money. They tore pages out of the script—so we finished early and without certain scenes!"

The story is set in 1876 and is about Cavalry Captain Phillip Donlin (Lloyd Bridges) who must lead his troops to Little Big Horn in time to warn General Custer of the attack the Sioux plan against him. Desperation leads Capt. Donlin to push his men hard. There is trouble on the home front for the captain as his wife Celie, whom Marie plays, is in a romance with Lieutenant John Haywood (John Ireland).

Little Big Horn opened to overwhelmingly positive reviews. Writing for *The Tidings* of Los Angeles, California, a reviewer described it as "a thoroughly professional job despite more emphasis on characterization than action." It elaborated, "Personal interest is built up around rival officers who feud over a woman (Marie Windsor) and concluded, "Adults who like a rugged tale, well told, may find it interesting." Writing for *The Los Angeles Times*, Philip K. Scheuer praised it as "one of those intimate, under-keyed, organic westerns about a crisis in the lives of some 15 men." Scheuer gave a special plaudit to director Charles Marquis Warren, calling him "an interesting addition to the ranks of directors" and noting that he "knows his Army and his West." The reviewer observes that Warren is able to build "suspense and some humor out of subplots involving the men" as well as making good use of the conflict over the "discontented wife" Marie played. A review published in *The Courier-Journal* of Louisville, Kentucky by Boyd Martin was similarly complimentary. It was headlined "'Little Big Horn' Tells Intense Story of Custer." Martin asserted, "There is a great deal of unusual suspense in *Little Big Horn*." It said sorties in the film "slow up the advance but never the action, for each episode has its own dramatic wallop." Martin also states that the love triangle of which Marie's character is apex "provides a tenseness" between the two major male stars and calls to mind "the Biblical situation between King David and the general whose wife he coveted."

Instead of riding a horse and twirling a gun, Marie buccaneered on the high seas in the 1951 *Hurricane Island* as the pirate Jane Bolton. This motion picture was directed by Lew Landers, scripted by David Mathews, and shot in Supercinecolor. This adventure film was inspired by Ponce De Leon's famed quest for the Fountain of Youth.

Early in the story Ponce de Leon (Edgar Barrier) takes an arrow from an Indian bow. Badly sickened, he does little during most of the flick as his underling, Captain Carlos Montalvo, played by the handsome and bulky Jon Hall, searches for the fabled Fountain of Youth in the hopes it will restore the punch in Ponce. In the captain's quest, he runs into several troubles. Some come from rival tribal leaders Princess Maria (Karen Randle) and Okahla (Jo Gilbert). He is also bedeviled by pirates, including the notorious lady pirate Jane Bolton whom Marie plays.

Hurricane Island never strives to be great art. Its screenplay provides such clunkers as "Oh, women! Oodles of them!" It is an entertaining B-movie, picturesque and picaresque. Contemporary reviewers did not discourage potential audience members from seeing it. A review published in *The Philadelphia Inquirer* observed that *Hurricane Island* "offered excitement of a sort with plenty of fighting, blowing up of ships, a real [sic] hurricane and a miracle." The reviewer commented that Jane Bolton's "cold-blooded approach to the acquisition of wealth becomes softened under the romantic influence of Captain Montalvo, but not until she has caused much bloodshed between the Indians and white men." A newspaper in Orlando, Florida, the *Orlando Evening Star*, published a short review of the film asserting, "Complications arise when Hall and Miss Windsor become romantically involved." It elaborated that the flick boasted "fights, magic rites and torrid love scenes." A brief piece in a Canadian newspaper, *The Gazette*, that was published shortly after the film's release, reported that Jon Hall—and presumably others—faced special difficulties in donning heavy costumes in hot weather. The article noted that when "the thermometer registered a sizzling 106 degrees," the actor did his scenes in "a heavy black jersey undergarment down to his ankles, thigh length suede boots, buckskin-jacket, a 50-pound armored breastplate, a visored metal helmet" along with pistols "stuck in a huge leather belt" plus "a heavy sword dangling from his waist." Dedicated professional that Jon Hall was, the article stated that he "assumed a stoical attitude about the situation" and "performed in his usual manner."

Hurricane Island was not a big hit and Marie did not like it. She called it "a most inferior film," adding "which B pictures don't have to be!" However, Laura Wagner thought it "at least had some camp value" and believed Marie was "creditably and terrifically cast as a treacherous lady pirate."

That same year of 1951 saw Marie in the crime drama *Two Dollar Bettor*. Posters advertising the film were emblazoned with the confessions: "I bet! I stole! I killed!" As the old saying goes, "one thing leads to another" and a journey to anywhere, including Hades-on-earth, begins with a single step.

Bank employee and widowed father of two teenaged girls, John Hewitt (John Litel) has lived his life on the straight and narrow as a dedicated worker and a concerned and loving Dad... until the day he bets a measly $2 on a horse race. He wins big! Euphoric over his huge return, he falls straight into a gambling addiction. Needless to say, he inevitably loses. Almost as inevitably, he embezzles from the bank to cover his losses—sure he will soon win big and return the stolen funds with the bank none the wiser. Things do not work out the way he fantasizes they will—do they ever?—and he is soon desperate. Enter Marie's Mary Slate, the female half of a con artist pair. The oily psychopath persuades Hewitt to rip off the bank to the tune of $20,000 (a truly astronomical sum in 1951) because she has a tip that is guaranteed to win.

One of the strangest aspects of *Two-Dollar Bettor* is the way it glides between genres. Most is solidly crime drama territory but we regularly pay visits to the Hewitt home where his daughter and their many friends are often gathered to dance and flirt. In the latter scenes, we seem to be in one of those famous 1950s teen movies.

Marie's Mary Slate is not onscreen long but she is pivotal to the plot as she must persuade the protagonist that she can be trusted while at the same time letting the audience know that she is a dyed-in-the-wool bad-die. Luckily for the film, Marie possessed the skill to pull it off, appearing to *appear* wholesome even as she plays a nasty con artist.

A Film Fights Racism

10

A FILM RELEASED IN 1952 in which Marie played had larger cultural implications. That movie was *Japanese War Bride*. Catherine Turney wrote the screenplay from a story Anson Bond penned. King Vidor directed the movie. *Japanese War Bride* marked the debut on American screens of Shirley Yamaguchi. The film gave her the distinction of being the first female Asian performer to have a starring role in an American film that was actually shot in the United States. Much of this motion picture was filmed in Salinas, California during the summer of 1951. Principal locations included the well-known "Smith ranch" and the Salinas Golf and County Club. Filming was also done at the Salinas depot and at lettuce packing sheds in the area.

The film is about Jim Sterling (Don Taylor), a Korean War veteran who returns to California with his Japanese wife with him. The two of them met in a Japanese hospital where Yamaguchi's character, Tae Shimizu, was employed as a nurse.

The movie explores the prejudice and discrimination the inter-racial couple faces, not only from neighbors but even within Jim Sterling's own family—especially his deeply prejudiced sister, Fran, who is played by Marie Windsor.

The film starts with waves crashing against rocks. We see a sign reading, "Korea." There are battle sounds and wounded soldiers on the ground. One comes to consciousness. Then he is in the hospital. It is Jim Sterling attended by pretty Asian nurse Tai Shimizu.

Since Tai's father is deceased, Jim goes to Tai's grandfather Eitaro Shimizu (Philip Ahn) to ask blessing for their marriage. Grandpa Shimizu explains that, following custom, two monkeys must be sacrificed.

Jim does not want the animals killed and runs out of the residence. Tai approaches him to explain that the Japanese have no such monkey-sacrificing custom but Grandpa wanted to test Jim's feeling.

Jim and Tai wed. They return to the Sterling family ranch. Members of the Sterling family, including his mother Harriet Sterling (Louise Lorimer), his father Art Sterling (Cameron Mitchell), brother Ed Sterling (James Bell), and sister-in-law Fran Sterling (Marie) appear to politely welcome Tai into the family. There might be reasons other than racial prejudice why Fran would take a dislike to Tai as it is intimated that Fran had a crush on Jim back in high school. There is also a suggestion that neighbor Emily Shafer (Sybil Merritt) was enamored of Jim during their teenaged years.

There is a scene in which family friends Emily Shafer and her mother Milly Shafer (Kathleen Mulqueen) come to visit. Beneath surface politeness is a sense of tension. When Milly thinks Tai is out of earshot—of course Tai is not—the woman lashes out, "I don't see how you can speak to her… I hate them all!" Milly's son/Emily's brother was killed by the Japanese in World War II. Emily realizes that Tai had nothing to do with that death but Milly's view of the entire ethnic group has been warped by her grief.

In another scene, one taking place at a gathering/dance, drunken family friend Woody Blacker (George Wallace—no, not the famous at-one-time segregationist politician) assumes Tai was a "geisha girl." Jim apparently believes this assumption reflects ill on Tai and it throws him into a fury.

A family of Japanese ancestry lives nearby so Tai finds a certain level of support with adult siblings Emma Hasagawa (May Takasugi) and Shiro Hasagawa (Lane Nakano) and the senior citizen father known only as "Mr." Hasagawa (William Yokota).

Two are about to become three when Tai announces that she is pregnant (the word is not said due to the era). She gives birth to James Sterling Jr. Mom Sterling comments that the baby "has the Sterling mouth" and Fran caustically comments that the newcomer "certainly doesn't have the Sterling eyes."

An anonymous letter to Art Sterling makes an insulting suggestion about Tai and precipitates a crisis.

Despite Jim's genuine love for Tai, he lapses into stereotyping under stress, asking his wife, "Don't you people ever cry?" He storms out before he can see the tears flowing down Tai's face.

The rest of the movie seeks to find a resolution between the bigotry the couple faces and the love they have for each other plus the newcomer.

Commenting on her character in *Japanese War Bride*, Marie asserted that the racially prejudiced and jealous Fran Sterling was "the bitchiest dame I've ever played." Always striving to give a role her all, and hardly averse to doing her own stunt work, Marie did something in the making of this movie that caused her real pain. "I asked an actor to really slap me hard in a scene to make it more believable," she remembered. "One of us miscalculated and he hit me with the butt of his hand rather than the 'faking-it' way of letting the fingers go over the face." As a result, Marie suffered a slight jaw fracture!

When *Japanese War Bride* debuted in February, 1952 in Salinas, California—in which so much of it had been shot—the manager of the Fox Theater at which the film debuted issued a special invitation to any local women who actually were "Japanese war brides." As well as local residents who were used in the filming of the movie, to be his special guests at the film's Salinas premiere. The Salinas newspaper called *The Californian* stated that people in either category should contact theater manager Duncan Knowles so he could arrange their guest status.

Japanese War Bride received mixed reviews when it opened. Writing for *The Daily News* of New York City, Dorothy Masters faulted the film as having "not approached the subject with strict integrity." It noted that Marie's character causes a "crisis evilly contrived" but asserts that "it wouldn't have mattered if the bride had come from Topeka or Tunis or Tokyo" as a "jealous sister-in-law" can object to a bride of any background. However, Masters observes that the movie shows "plausible incidents of a minor caliber" that *are* directly linked to someone unable to "forget that her son was killed by the Japanese" and another character who drunkenly stereotypes Japanese woman as "geisha girls." Masters also writes, "All the roles are well played," singling out Don Taylor and Shirley Yamaguchi for special praise.

Writing for the *Los Angeles Times*, John L. Scott asserted, "Restraint in handling a controversial subject takes *Japanese War Bride*, a Bernhard production, out of the sensational class." Scott praises all the film's actors, saying they "fit into the story efficiently."

Japanese War Bride was similar to *The Teahouse of the August Moon* (1956) and *Sayonara* (1957), in focusing on a marriage between a Caucasian and an Asian. Some observers argued that this films helped decrease prejudice against such unions. In Sarah Kovner's book *Occupying Power:*

Sex Workers and Servicemen in Postwar Japan, she asserted, "The release of the 1952 motion picture *Japanese War Bride*—and the widespread posters that advertised the film made Japanese wives increasingly visible in the United States." Kovner continued that "other films such as the 1956 *Teahouse of the August Moon*" as well as "the 1957 *Sayonara*" increased tolerance because they "presented American audiences with sympathetic examples of interracial couples."

11

The Sniper, The Narrow Margin, Outlaw Women

ANOTHER 1952 FILM in which Marie played was the film noir entitled *The Sniper*. This film was the return of Edward Dmytryk, a victim of the notorious Red Scare, to directing. Dmytryk had been a member of the Communist Party for a very brief period and that had gotten him blacklisted and even briefly jailed for contempt of Congress. However, in 1951, he agreed to testify and named names. He left for England for a period before returning to the United States where Stanley Kramer, acting in capacity of producer, hired Dmytryk to direct *The Sniper*. Arthur Franz stars as anti-hero Eddie Miller who earns his living making deliveries. He also struggles with a deep-seated antagonism toward women. He is especially angry at women he finds attractive. Dark-haired women in their twenties are "his type."

Eventually the disturbed man begins shooting women with an M1 carbine.

Marie is only in the film for less than ten minutes as she plays first victim, bar pianist Jean Darr. She is around enough for the audience to care about Jean. She is no prima donna of arrogance and temper tantrums but a pleasant, cheerful, and kindly woman. Eddie comes to Jean's home to make a delivery of a dress from a cleaning service. When she realizes his hand is bandaged, she expresses concern and sympathy. The phone rings and a male friend wants to visit her. She asks that Eddie leave so the other man "won't get any wrong ideas." Eddie obligingly leaves—but he is enraged at the reminder that he is not Jean's suitor.

The actress who performed stunts in Westerns that most actresses would have left to stunt workers wanted to actually *play* the piano when her character played. Thus, she devoted a month and a half to taking piano lessons. She learned the compositions used in *The Sniper* and her fingers were actually tickling them out on the ivories in the piano scenes. Nevertheless, as is often done, the music was in fact dubbed. Still, it is likely her dedication lent these scenes an authenticity they might not otherwise have possessed.

The dramatic scene in which she is shot and her head strikes a pane of glass, shattering it, certainly looks dangerous. However, Marie told an interviewer that it held no real-life terror. "I wasn't worried about being hurt because the glass was prop-glass made out of sugar, I think. I choreographed what I would do and did it in one take."

Still another 1952 film noir, *The Narrow Margin* by RKO Pictures, would prove to be one of Marie's greatest achievements in cinema. It would also lead directly to her casting in another, equally remarkable, motion picture.

The Narrow Margin was directed by Richard Fleischer. Earl Felton wrote its screenplay based on a story penned by Martin Goldsmith and Jack Leonard. It was shot in only 15 days with the train interiors on an RKO soundstage and the exterior station scenes shot in the Los Angeles Union Station. The movie stars Charles McGraw as Detective Sergeant Walter Brown of the Los Angeles Police Department (LAPD). Brown has been assigned to protect Marie Windsor's character, whom they know as Mrs. Frankie Neall, the widow of a notorious gangster. She is supposed to travel from Chicago to Los Angeles to testify before a grand jury. Other gangsters want to stop her from testifying and they also want to get their hands on the "payoff list" her husband bequeathed to her.

Prior to meeting the widow Neall, Brown's partner and pal Sergeant Gus Forbes (Don Beddoe) are riding in a car when Forbes asks Brown what to expect from her. Brown describes her as a classic noir femme fatale: "She's the sixty-cent special. Cheap. Flashy. Strictly poison under the gravy." Felton's screenplay includes a lot of classically "tough" talk.

Most of the film's story takes place in a train, a common setting for cinema crime stories. As Rob Nixon writes, "Trains have always served filmmakers as a terrific background for suspense thrillers." Alfred Hitchcock made several motion pictures that featured such settings including the aptly titled *Strangers on a Train* (1952). Nixon believes much of the strength of *The Narrow Margin* is due to the way "director Richard Fleischer exploits the narrow corridors and cramped compartments to maximum effect, heightening the sense of claustrophobia and paranoia of being trapped without an exit." An interesting characteristic of the film is that it lacks a soundtrack in the usual sense of the term. There is no music score. Rather, the sound of a train is played at dramatic junctures in the story. Although not musically scored, music is heard when Marie's character plays it on her phonograph.

A major part of what makes *The Narrow Margin* a stunning drama is the way Marie Windsor and Charles McGraw play off each other. When Brown and Forbes first encounter "Mrs. Frankie Neal," she is relaxing by a phonograph. She flings back her hair and follows her protectors out of her room. Then she has a small accident as her necklace breaks, sending white beads scattering hither and yon. Perhaps this little, seemingly meaningless accident is emblematic of the possibility of more meaningful, even tragic, accidents—a possibility that hovers over all our characters.

As the group leaves the room in which Marie's character has been staying, the audience sees a man in shadow with a gun. Before they get very far, this man, a gangster named Densel (Peter Virgo), steps out of the shadows and shoots, killing Forbes. Brown chases the murderer only to get tangled in lines of clothing hung out to dry. "Some protection!" Mrs. Neal sniffs sarcastically.

Once Brown and Mrs. Frankie Neall are in the train, a sense of claustrophobia heightens the tensions which are doubly heightened by the nasty interchanges between the police officer and the woman he guards.

Brown runs into a woman with a young child. She is a bright and wholesome blonde whom he knows as Ann Sinclair (Jacqueline White) and her rambunctious little boy is Tommy (Gordon Gebert). She seems quite a contrast to the hardened character played by Marie.

At one point, it seems that gangsters searching for Mrs. Frankie Neall have mistaken Mrs. Sinclair for the gangster's widow—a situation that suits Marie's character just fine as it puts her out of danger. "Sister, I've known some pretty hard cases in my time but you make them all look like putty," Brown says. When she seems nonplussed by the possibility that another woman (Jacqueline White) could take a bullet meant for her, he tells her she makes him want to lose his lunch. "Use your own sink!" she snaps.

Brown is "put to the test" in an odd way when gangster Vincent Yost (Peter Brocco) tries to get the detective to give up the identity of Neall's widow. He tells Brown a big hunk of money would follow—which he could even use quite honorably to aid the widow and children of his dead partner. Even though Brown despises the woman he guards, he has been sworn to uphold the law and rejects the offer. He would like to arrest Yost for bribery but cannot because the offer was made outside Brown's juris-diction.

The Narrow Margin has an interesting trick up its sleeve. The woman said to be mistaken for Mrs. Frankie Neall *is* Mrs. Frankie Neall. And the tough-as-nails character played by Marie Windsor? She is an undercover police officer! Brown also learns that he was not told her true identity because superiors wanted to make sure that Brown was not corrupt.

There is an odd parallel in this subterfuge with Marie Windsor's actual life. In *The Narrow Margin*, we meet a woman who seems to embody lawlessness but who is actually an agent of the law. The actress Marie Windsor often played callous and nasty characters; the person named Marie Windsor was a sensitive and deeply ethical individual, a kind of "sheep in wolf's clothing" as one reporter described her.

Marie's character and Charles McGraw's sniped at each other on-screen but this hardly characterized the real life relationship of the two performers. Marie thought McGraw "was a sweetheart… a very sweet man." She remembered him as having "alcohol problems" but, as far as she recalled, "He didn't drink on set."

While making *The Narrow Margin*, Marie suffered a pain that was far more than she expected. She was thrown against the seat in the train. She was supposed to have her head slam into the upholstered part but instead it hit the wood frame. "It really stunned me but was good for the scene," Marie stated.

Marie is reported to have told an odd story about how she was cast in *The Narrow Margin*: "My agent climbed through the [office] window of the casting director with a test that I had made out at 20th Century Fox—and that was it." She was impressed by the attention and plaudits the movie received. "We certainly made a lot of noise with that picture," Marie commented. "It ran with all the top pictures and we got all the reviews."

The Narrow Margin was a hit with both critics and audiences. Martin Goldsmith and Jack Leonard were nominated for an Academy Award in the Best Writing, Motion Picture Story category. An American Film Institute (AFI) article on the film states, "Reviewers praised the picture's tautness and imaginative camera angles." It further observed that film historians often cite it as "a quintessential example of the film noir genre." A Turner Classic Movies (TCM) piece on *The Narrow Margin* praises Marie for bringing just the right amount of sexy sass to the flick: "A certain degree of the film's popularity should also be credited to its female star,

Marie Windsor, the B-movie queen with the killer body and bedroom eyes…. Her role in this film as the gangland widow with a few secrets of her own was one of the best of her career."

While acting in *The Narrow Margin*, Marie made friends with its producer, Stanley Rubin, and they would stay friends over the year. Although Marie was never to again work with director Richard Fleischer, she praised him in an interview. "He was a darling man," she asserted.

A 1952 motion picture in which Marie starred entitled *Outlaw Women* was a most eccentric Western. As an IMDb user reviewer observed, the plethora of Westerns Hollywood has churned out has led some filmmakers to strain for gimmicks to make a movie of the genre stand out. That reviewer cited a 1938 Western entitled *The Terror of Tiny Town* in which all the performers in the Wild West were dwarves. The same individual also cited the 1937 "race film" *Harlem on the Prairie* in which all the performers were what was then called "colored" or "Negroes." *Outlaw Women* has as its gimmick a town run by females. The motion picture does *not* have a female-only cast but the idea of a "women's town" is certainly an unusual gimmick. This writer does not see the flick as "feminist" as some observers do but just as having a concept designed to set it apart from other Westerns. *Outlaw Women* was far more gimmicky than social/political as seen in the advertisements that clearly appealed to male interest with the tagline, "Six Gun Sirens Who Shoot To Thrill!" Another ad boasted: "Meet the Babes Who Put the *Bad* in the Bad Men!"

Orville H. Hampton wrote the screenplay for *Outlaw Women* and Sam Newfield and Ron Omond directed it. It was filmed in Cinecolor. Marie starred as "Iron Mae" McLeod who controls the town of Las Mujeres (Spanish for "The Women") and owns its gambling casino. Men can enter the town if they have a special reason or are employed by it. And despite the premise, there really is no shortage of the male gender in this Western as Pluto Billy (Jackie Coogan) shows up to be a miner, Woody Callaway (Richard Rober) appears to gamble, and Dr. Ridgeway (Allan Nixon) is needed to tend wounds and ills. Indeed, Iron Mae's associate, Beth Larabee (Carla Balenda) actually kidnaps the good doctor! There is a suggestion she needs a man for… well, that she needs a man. Another of the town's notable rowdy lady Larabees is Ellen Larabee (Jacqueline Fontaine).

Trouble comes big time in the form of gang leader Frank Slater (Richard Avonde) who wants to muscle in on the gambling there. Iron Mae does not cotton to the idea of partnering with Slater and women start getting murdered. Since women cannot vote even in Las Mujeres—this is the 19th century after all—Woody Callaway becomes the marshal and restores both law and order. He even manages to win the affections of Iron Mae.

When *Outlaw Women* was released, the *Kenosha News* of Kenosha, Wisconsin ran a brief article focusing on Kenosha native Jacqueline Fontaine who made a "colorful film bow" in the Western. It continued, "The blond singer runs the gamut of characterization in the western feature. When she's not vocalizing a sultry number clad in mesh hose and a glamorous gown, she's out on the range in riding habit and mask, holding up stagecoaches." A contemporary review in *The Times* of Shreveport, Louisiana reported that the film "brings a new wrinkle to westerns. Its premise is a western town, controlled by a woman and run by women." It quoted an unnamed film editor describing the females in the film as "the roughest set of chicks you'd want to see." The article said, "These belles of the brawl are superb."

Marie remembered an odd experience during the making of *Outlaw Women*: "The makeup man was Carlie Taylor. I went to the makeup department and sat there a little while. Finally, he asked what color makeup did I want. I applied the makeup myself. When I finished, someone asked for me. Until then, Carlie didn't know *I* was the *star!*"

Sci-Fi Sorties

12

THE JUNGLE WAS THE TITLE of a motion picture Marie starred in that was also released in 1952. Filmed in sepia, it was a combination of a foreign adventure and science fiction film. She was once again a princess, as she had been in *Outpost in Morocco*, but this time a princess of India. Carroll Young is credited for writing the movie's screenplay while Orville Hampton is credited for having written some of its dialogue. William Berke directed it. The opening credits relate, "This picture was photographed entirely in India in the cities, the villages and… The Jungle." Marie plays the Indian Princess Mari and Cesar Romero appears as an Indian named Rama Singh. Rod Cameron is cast as the white hunter Steve Bentley. There are also "real" Indians playing Indians: Sulochana plays Aunt Sumira, M. N. Nambiar plays Mahaji, Ramakrishna plays Babu, and Chitra Devi appears as a dancer.

Author Mark David Welsh asserts that *The Jungle* is "far more interesting for the circumstances of its making than the final results." How so? An Indian producer wanted to "shoot an adventure movie on location with local crews but import American names to star, write, and direct." To that end, he partnered with American producer Robert L. Lippert.

The tale of *The Jungle* starts with Princess Mari returning to India after a sojourn in the West. Her royal father is seriously ill and hospitalized. She is disturbed by odd incidents occurring in rural areas. Animals, especially elephants, are causing havoc with stampedes. Steve Bentley tells her of a team of hunters he led, all of whom—except himself—were killed by elephants. (One of those who died was the brother of Rama Singh). Steve also tells Princess Mari of a surprising reason the elephants are running, claiming they have panicked because of even larger animals. Those larger animals are none other than wooly mammoths, the ancestors of the modern elephant. Princess Mara scoffs. Everyone knows wooly mammoths died out in the Ice Age!

Our major characters are soon off to investigate the reasons for the elephant stampede. Except for Steve, they expect to find something a bit more reasonable than wooly mammoths. During the excursion, there is a certain romantic tension between Steve and Princess Mara which, naturally enough, sets off jealousy in Rama Singh who has long expected to marry her. The audience sees many scenes of a cute monkey cutting cute antics as well as scenes of animals fighting each other. These scenes are of special interest and set the flick apart from others like it. As Mark David Welsh notes, "We get impressive landscapes, lots of extras, and genuine wildlife and animal shots as opposed to the usual tired library footage." There is also a special aura radiated by the sepia cinematography, a brown and white filming that recalls Victoria-era photographs and tintypes. In this writer's opinion, sepia lends a fable-like quality to this story much as the unusual cinematography of *Hellfire* gave to that film.

When survivors from past eras are featured in movies, they are usually dinosaurs so *The Jungle* is notable in giving us pre-historic mammals. When they finally appear, it is pretty obvious that they are modern elephants covered with hairy carpets and sporting fake super-tusks but they are fun to watch.

Marie's acting was, as usual, top-notch and Cesar Romero gave an excellent performance as well. This author found Rod Cameron's performance rather one-note but it was hardly embarrassing.

According to Mark David Welsh, Marie was troubled during part of the making of the film because the fight staged between tiger and bear "disgusted Windsor so much that she considered reporting the filmmakers for animal cruelty." Since her childhood, Marie held animals dear so it is natural that even the slightest suggestion of animal cruelty would offend her. Perhaps it was because of her obvious affection for animals that the producer of the film offered her a monkey as a gift. Rod Cameron's wife wanted the furry creature, Marie continued, and "she made such a fuss, because she wanted it, that I finally said, 'Take it!'" The monkey turned out to be a mixed blessing for its owner. "She had a terrible time getting it into the United States," Marie disclosed. "And it messed up her house pretty bad!"

Windsor's son, Rick Hupp, told this author that his mother took photographs and film of what she considered animal cruelty on the set of *The*

Jungle and was made to surrender both pictures and film at the airport before she left India. "The Indian authorities wouldn't let her take it out of the country," Hupp recalled.

1952 was also the year in which Dwight David "Ike" Eisenhower ran for the presidency on the Republican ticket against Democrat Adlai Stevenson. Marie was a lifelong Republican and, like many others, "I Like Ike" described her leanings that year and she campaigned and made appearances on Eisenhower's behalf.

Marie played a major role in the 1953 science fiction movie *Cat-Women of the Moon*. Sonny Tufts was first in the credits, Victor Jory second, and Marie third. Despite its title, the film was not a comedy. Indeed, there was not a deliberately funny line in the film. However, it was just as silly and kitschy as the title suggests. It would also prove unexpectedly influential.

Sonny Tufts, led a peculiar life. It began in a promising manner when he was born Bowen Charlton "Sonny" Tufts III in 1911 into a wealthy Boston family. The privileged Tufts graduated from Yale University in 1935. His first love was opera and he auditioned at New York's Metropolitan Opera. Then he switched to popular music and the Broadway stage.

In the early 1940s he headed to Hollywood where he almost instantly enjoyed success in comedies. He was not particularly gifted as an actor but a deficit of available males during the time period worked to favor his career. A college football injury left him 4-F so while other male performers were risking their lives to save the world from Nazi Germany, Fascist Italy, and Imperial Japan, the handsome blonde and muscular Sonny Tufts was in hot demand as one of the few macho men available for movie acting.

As the 1940s wound down, so did Tufts's career. He started garnering negative publicity for foolish actions in his private life. In 1950 and 1951, the actor was arrested three times on charges of public intoxication. One of those arrests occurred after Tufts was found passed-out on a Sunset Strip sidewalk. In a truly outrageous incident, he was at a coffee shop with a hula dancer when he got into a physical fight about his $4.65 dinner bill. On another occasion, a stripper sued him for allegedly biting her thigh so deeply he left it permanently disfigured. The suit was settled out of court. Soon after that off lawsuit was settled, a nightclub dancer sued him, again for a bite that she said left a permanent scar. In 1955, only two years after starring in *Cat-Women of the Moon*, he was arrested on the complaint of a woman claiming he had pinched and bitten her in a restaurant.

An urban legend attached itself to Tufts. The legend claims that the actor Joseph Cotton had just completed a radio show episode when he was handed a paper giving information about who would perform the next week. Reading it cold, it is related that he said, "The episode for next week will feature that fine actor—SONNY TUFTS?!"

In fact, this never occurred. This author happens to be an Old Time Radio fan. I listened to Cotton say, after his own performance in a radio episode, that he hoped the audience would tune in next week "when Sonny Tufts will be…" There was no sarcasm or irony in the statement. But the story gained currency because it seemed plausible.

Cat-Women of the Moon was directed by Arthur Hill from a screenplay penned by Roy Hamilton. In the screen credits, Marie is listed third, after Sonny Tufts and Victor Jory. Susan Morrow, cat-women leader Alpha, is listed above and at the same time as with Douglas Fowley and Bill Phipps while the other cat-women are listed as "The Hollywood Cover Girls," a title probably meant to emphasize their sensual beauty.

The movie begins with a voiceover musing about how humans have long yearned to explore the "eternal wonders of space and time." Instead of making such discoveries in the future, the narrator asks, "Why not now?"

We see a spaceship apparently launched into outer space. Then we are inside the spaceship. The crew consists of four men and a woman: Sonny Tufts as Laird Grainger, Victor Jory as Kim Reissner, William Phipps as Doug Smith, Douglas Fowley as Walt Walters, and Marie Windsor as Helen Salinger. The crew appears to be resting. Then they get up. The femininity of the one female member of the crew is emphasized when Marie as Helen Salinger takes out a compact and combs her hair. There is something striking about a "space woman" primping as soon as she gets into outer space! However, Helen Salinger is not on this spaceship as a plaything for the men, nor is she there to perform domestic duties such as cooking and cleaning. Helen has a very responsible and non-stereotypical role as the ship's navigator. The leader of the space ship is Laird Granger, who is played by Sonny Tufts. But it is the navigator who sets the course for the moon's dark side.

Once there, Marie seems a bit disgruntled, peevishly complaining in her spacesuit, "These shoes are too heavy." The group of moon explorers take along cigarettes and a "just-in-case" firearm. The moon turns out to be a surprising place as it has an atmosphere so our heroes and our heroine can divest themselves of the helmets. They also use the gun as visits to moon caves bring them close to two spiders, each of which is about the size of a small car. "I loved that spider, I loved all the special effects things," Marie said about the film. However, the enormous spider caused problems for the crew. "They had a terrible time getting it mechanically to work!" Marie commented.

After destroying the spiders, we find that there is intelligent life on the moon. That life is made up of pretty ladies wearing tight-fitting black outfits with their hair in beehives that are pulled "back" rather than "up" as in typical earth beehive fashion. "Cat-women" may refer to the eye makeup they wear that suggests feline orbs. We soon learn that something went wrong in the environment years before that caused moon men to die off. We also learn that the cat-women are telepathic and can insert thoughts into humans. They concentrate on Helen because her being of their gender makes this trick easier for them to perform. They are conspiring to make Helen lead them to earth where they hope to rule the planet.

The film's shoestring budget shows in its poor sets with both outer space and the moonscape obviously drawings (albeit rather pretty drawings). Marie was understandably not proud of the film, calling it "one of the worst pictures I was ever in." She was negatively impressed by the major props chosen for the spaceship. "We were traveling to the moon seated in desk chairs with wheels on the bottom!" she incredulously observed. "We were strapped into those chairs and off we went into outer space! And I thought, 'Gee, can't they figure out that these chairs would be rolling and floating around? It was so silly!"

It opened to mixed reviews. A brief, indeed one paragraph *New York Times* review observed that the moon's cat-women "try to get their hands on the visitors' rocket ship, hoping to come down here and hypnotize us all." It sarcastically concludes, "Considering the delegation that went up, it's hard to imagine why." A kinder *Variety* review asserted that the "cast ably portray their respective roles" and elaborated, "Arthur Hilton makes his direction count in catching the spirit of the theme, and art direction is far above average for a film of this caliber."

Although Marie was correct in calling the flick "silly," it has become a cult classic of the "so-bad-it's-good" variety. Marie realized that much of the film was "so ridiculous" but observed that "it sure became a film buff's favorite." Part of the reason for its cult status is silliness played completely seriously. Perhaps another is the presence of Marie Windsor. Despite the cringing clinker of a script, she manages to play navigator

Helen in a skillfully nuanced manner as she shifts from committed professional to traditionally vain female to peevish complainer to victim of mind control.

Cat-Women of the Moon not only possesses a cult following but a real place in film history. The *Encyclopedia of Science Fiction* calls it "one of the most influential science fiction films ever made" because it launched (pun intended) a series of motion pictures about encounters between we earthlings and planets of all-female or mostly-female humanoid types like the also campily titled *Fire Maidens from Outer Space* (1956) and *Voyage to the Planet of the Prehistoric Women* (1968). The *Encyclopedia of Science Fiction* observed that the first film with the scenario of an earth space ship landing on a planet without men was *Abbott and Costello Go To Mars* (1953) which was released a few months before *Cat-Women of the Moon.* The *Encyclopedia of Science Fiction* elaborates that *Cat-Women of the Moon* established the patterns that other similar films followed.

Continuing Achievements

13

MARIE PLAYED IN FIVE OTHER motion pictures released in 1953: *The Tall Texan*, *Trouble Along the Way*, *City That Never Sleeps*, *So This Is Love*, and *The Eddie Cantor Story*.

In *The Tall Texan*, Sheriff Chadbourne (Samuel Herrick) is transporting suspect Ben Trask (Lloyd Bridges) in a covered wagon to El Paso. Other passengers in the wagon are sea captain Theodore Bess (Lee J. Cobb) and married couple Jerry (Dean Train) and Laura (Marie Windsor). Early in the journey, the group encounters a wounded American Indian who has been banished by his tribe. The tribe attacks the wagon. Needing as many to defend the wagon as possible, the Sheriff releases Ben from his handcuffs so he can wield a gun at the attacking Indians. The Indians wound Sheriff Chadbourne and kill Jerry. Although Ben would like to escape, he helps the sea captain free the sheriff who has become trapped under the overturned wagon. The injured Indian offers to lead the people in the wagon to a place that he claims has gold. He displays a gold nugget. A trader named Joshua Tinnen (Luther Adler) soon appears. He takes the liberty of going through the wagon and its contents. In a bag belonging to Theodore Bess, Joshua discovers papers indicating Bess had his captain's license pulled. The group agrees to let Tinnen share in any gold discovery if he allows them the use of his horses and supplies. Laura has little time to grieve as the group is soon off on a hunt for the precious metal. She also finds herself in the midst of a love triangle, fighting off the aggressive Theodore Bess and falling for Ben Trask—who we learn is suspected of murdering his own brother. His stout denials and the overall depiction of his character leads the audience to feel that this is a case of a fellow falsely accused. Ben Trask is the "tall Texan" of the title. An IMDb review remarks that the title is a bit inappropriate as Lloyd Bridges, at six feet tall, is only a few inches taller than the average man.

The Tall Texan has been described by more than one commentator as combining elements of *Stagecoach* and *Treasure of the Sierra Madre*. Samuel Roeca penned the script for *The Tall Texan* with Elizabeth Reinhardt credited for putting in "additional dialogue." The motion picture was directed by Elmo Williams. It was Williams' first foray into directing after his triumph as film editor on the 1952 Gary Cooper classic *High Noon*. Williams won an Academy Award for his *High Noon* editing. One interesting aspect of *The Tall Texan* is the way it tries to balance the conflict between the whites and the Indians. At one point, Joshua Tinnen asks, "How do we know we can trust the Indians to keep their word?" "You got a point there," Ben Trask acknowledges. "Indians got a point, too. They've had dealings with whites before." *The Salt Lake Tribune* published a contemporary review headlined, "Tall Texan Packed With Emotions." The article stated, "Long, lean and lethal, Lloyd Bridges tops an able cast." Another contemporary review, one published in *The Los Angeles Times*, wrote, "The oats-and-corn drama seems to have taken a shot in the arm if *The Tall Texan* is any criterion." That review praised the movie "quality in both story and the clarity and earthiness of its character drawing." It noted that the story is filled with quarrels, greedy intrigues and death" and that the performers "all play their roles vividly."

Commenting on *The Tall Texan*, Marie disclosed, "We did that in New Mexico, in an area where the dust was so fine that when we drove out to location, we'd be covered in this fine dust even if the windows were rolled up tight. It was very, very dusty."

Oddly enough, *The Tall Texan* played a role in a little contest held in Denton, Texas. The *Denton Record-Chronicle* reported on a limerick contest that was held; its winners got a pair of guest tickets to see *The Tall Texan*. The article did not say how many entered the contest but reported that no less than twelve individuals won! A sample limerick (I do not know whether or not it won): "The Tall Texan is long and lean/He's in the best show on the screen."

Trouble Along the Way was a comedy-drama that brought Marie together with John Wayne again. Michael Curtiz directed the film. The screenplay was written by Jack Rose, Melville Shavelson, and the uncredited James Edward Grant. The movie appears to have run into "trouble along the way" of its making. Author Jeremy Arnold reported, "Originally titled *Alma Mater*, this was writer Melville Shavelson's first film as producer, and he was less than thrilled to have the experience marred by a serious run-in with Wayne. The issue was the screenplay. Wayne had previously told Shavelson that while he liked the script, he wanted to bring in writer James Edward Grant for a polish—because, as Wayne put it, Grant 'has kind of a good feeling for my way of talking.' Horrified at the thought of any script tampering, Shavelson tried to persuade Wayne not to do this—successfully, he thought. But Wayne went ahead and had Grant secretly rewrite dialogue for several characters. Unable to reign in the biggest star in the world, Shavelson then had the bright idea of shooting two scripts: Wayne's version when Wayne was working and the 'real' version when the star wasn't around."

Inevitably, the plan backfired. "Duke showed up on a day he wasn't supposed to be there and found out what was going on," Shavelson glumly recalled. Infuriated, the superstar gave Shavelson an energetic dressing-down. Each man vowed he would never work with the other again—and they never did. Jeremy Arnold speculates, "The resulting film's uneven pace was probably due to the competing scripts and was also a big reason it didn't fare well at the box office." Shavelson suggested another reason that film was not a hit: "There wasn't a horse in the picture."

The tale of *Trouble Along the Way* begins with the film showing a college that we learn was founded way back in 1873. Set in its contemporary era, the small religious institution of St. Anthony's College is in dire financial straits. The elderly rector Father Burke (Charles Coburn) is informed by his superiors that, unless it can pull itself out of debt within about a year, the school will be closed. Ever the optimist, Father Burke believes "God will find a way" to save St. Anthony's College. The instrument of God's way, Father Burke himself, believes a winning football team is the ticket to "saving" the college and he finds Steve Williams, played by Wayne, a man who was once a winning football coach although he has recently fallen on hard times (reminiscent of the situation of St. Anthony's College). Steve is dismissive of the idea but eagerly accepts it when he is informed that ex-wife Anne (Marie) seeks custody of the couple's 11-year-old daughter Carole (Sherry Jackson).

Huh? Whaaa—? In a film made and set in 1953, a couple have broken up and *Dad* has custody of a kid? We are shown in flashback that Steve "caught" Anne with the fellow who is now her new hubby. What's more, and worse, Steve and Anne did not divorce but had their marriage annulled. It seems Anne did not keep good track of things and had failed to get a divorce from her first husband! Even with these givens, courts in that period would have strongly favored a Mom who wanted custody of her child but it appeared Anne simply did not have much interest in little Carole. Steve, who was an unusually active Dad for the time period, *did* want his child.

Has Anne's long dormant mothering instinct kicked in after about a decade? The film does not make her motives all that clear but we are given to think this could be a ruse to get Steve back in her life. In their few scenes together, Anne shows only a modicum of interest in Carole.

A social worker, Alice Singleton (Donna Reed), is assigned to look into the case and make a report on it. Complications ensue as Steve and Alice find themselves increasingly attracted to each other. Indeed, there are scenes in which Steve commits what would be recognized today—and possibly even at the time—as an assault when he grabs Alice and kisses her. However, this was only-a-movie and John Wayne followed a script. Even though Alice is falling in love with Steve, she has a bias on Anne's side due to her own background. Alice was a "daddy's girl" who grew up with tomboy ways and had trouble fitting into the "women's world" of the time as a consequence.

Steve has his work cut out for him at St. Anthony's College in trying to whip up a good football team in a limited time framework and is quite strained by having to put out fires on two fronts. Nevertheless, this is a flick starring John Wayne so we have a sense things will have to turn out well in the end. A contemporary review published in *Variety* praised *Trouble Along the Way* as "a delightful comedy-drama" and asserted, "The lines, a principle factor in carrying the film, are zinged home by the performers under the neat directorial timing of Michael Curtiz, who also mixed in a nice touch of sentiment." That review continued, "John Wayne is completely at home in a role that, while action-ful in most phases, leans toward a humorous lightness. Charles Coburn wallops dialog lines delightfully incongruous to the priest character he plays. Donna Reed gives her role as a probation officer all that it needs." The reviewer called Sherry Jackson's performance as the daughter a "standout." Marie had few scenes and the ones she was in were undemanding as they basically called for her to look attractive (easily done by this beauty) and be unsympathetic (ditto). However, she did run into a bit of "trouble along the way" when filming her scenes (sorry, I could not resist). The scene called for her to pick up ice cubes with tongs and put them into a glass. It was hard for her to get this done correctly and Curtis yelled, "How can you be so stupid! Haven't you ever used those ice things before?" However, Marie added that this was the *only* time Curtiz yelled at her during the film's making.

Directed by John H. Auer and written by Steve Fisher, *City That Never Sleeps* is a fascinatingly eccentric film noir. "I am the city," a voice (Chill Wills) tells us as we see a scan of various buildings nestled together. The voiceover continues that it is "part of America" and a "melting pot of every race, creed, color, and religion in humanity." It tells us that it will tell the story of "just one night" in the city identified as Chicago. The voice invites us to "meet my citizens." He introduces "Greg Warren (Wally Cassell), a mechanical mime" in a store window who was once an actor. The "Mechanical Man" is among the most striking images in the film as his face is covered in shiny make-up designed to make him look like a machine. He has white gloves on his hands and obvious strings attached to him as he stands in a store window and moves his body robotically. We are introduced to Johnny Kelly (Gig Young), "a man who has reached a crisis" in his life as both police officer and husband. Then there is Sally (Mala Powers), who has "the face of an angel" but works "dancing in a nightclub." The film shows us a scene between Johnny and Sally or "Angel Face." Johnny is a married man and wants to leave wife Kathy to run off with Sally and start a fresh life elsewhere. We learn that Kathy had dreams of being a "shining star" but is reduced to a job filled with "sweat and leering eyes." She quit her job and the nightclub has hired a replacement. Cut to a scene through a window of a rabbit in a cage and the voiceover saying, "This is another one of my citizens" but adds "no, not him" of the rabbit. Rather, the citizen is the man who removes the bunny from its enclosure. The voice tells us, "Hayes Stewart (William Talman) started out in his youth to become a magician… talented with his fingers" he started "picking pockets" before becoming an overall "hoodlum." Then we go to "brilliant attorney" Penrod Biddel (Edward Arnold) with his "lovely young wife Lydia (Marie)." The lawyer is in a large room being interviewed by the press. Although the phrase "young wife" is used, Marie was in fact in her early thirties when she made this film but she also looked a bit younger.

The voiceover leaves off and we are back with Johnny Kelly who is chatting with his father, also a cop, Sergeant John "Pop" Kelly Sr. (Otto Hulett). His father asks him about his job and Johnny sarcastically replies, "It's making me filthy rich." Pop points out he has a good wife who loves him and Johnny retorts, "She loves her job." Pop is clearly distressed by his son's attitudes.

Johnny Kelly learns that his regular partner is out sick so he has a temporary replacement in Sergeant Joe (also Chill Wills).

Soon Johnny is meeting with Penrod Biddell at the latter's swank residence. This is where Marie has her first "real" or talking scene. "Darling!" she calls, drawing Penrod into another room. She explains that she is going to visit a friend of hers named Helen and she wanted Penrod in a room alone with her so she could give him a kiss before exiting. She is utterly loving and affectionate to Penrod who is equally so with her.

In his wife's absence, Penrod lets Johnny know the attorney has a major problem in a crook named Hayes Stewart. Penrod is informed that Johnny is planning to steal from Penrod's safe. The big shot wants Johnny to pick Hayes up and then transport him to Indiana where he can be jailed for manslaughter. It's an "off-the-books" case so Johnny wants no part of it—until Penrod tells the cop that Hayes has been palling around with a fellow named Stubby. Johnny is in. Later we learn that Stubby is Johnny's younger brother.

Scenes follow of Hayes discovering in a very bitter manner that Penrod is onto his scheme.

Another scene has Kathy (Paula Raymond) talking with her father-in-law about woes in the marriage. "It's my fault, Pop," she explains. "I make more money than he does." She says that can "eat on a man" so she will quit her job to save his pride. Interestingly, the film comments on gender roles more than once. Since this is the 1950s, the clear model is husband-breadwinner and dependent housewife. Nevertheless, there are problems with this model. At one point, someone asks Johnny if he and Kathy have kids and he rhetorically asks, "On my salary?" But the couple's income is soon to be cut by more than half when Kathy quits paid work for full-time housewifery. Of course, a housewife has more time to bargain shop and look for ways to take advantage of coupons as well as to save money in other ways like mending clothes.

Greg Warren, Johnny's rival for Sally's affections, wants her to join him in a comedy act that has a "switch" as its basis with the husband as the nag.

Having seen Lydia "properly" affectionate with her husband, there is a bit of surprise in the next scene when she calls another man "darling" and, in her most sensuous and seductive voice, asks, "What is better than money?" She answers, "The black magic of Hayes Stewart. Darling, give me some magic."

In a three-way confrontation—Penrod, Hayes, and Lydia—we learn that Lydia was running a cash register and waiting tables in a cheap restaurant when Penrod met her. Like Sally, Lydia was happy to quit her paid work for being a housewife. However, her past was a problem in their marriage as her husband often reminded her of how humble her previous life had been.

The movie shows us a good deal more in violence and bloodshed before bestowing an ultimately happy ending—or, at least, one as happy as it can be after the loss of lives. In a 1953 review published in *The Lincoln Star* of Lincoln, Nebraska, Joe Fitz Gerald called *City That Never Sleeps* a "spine-tingling action drama which builds for taut suspense in an atmosphere of big city color and excitement." Gerald continues, "The thriller presents a vivid and sometimes lurid cross-section of Chicago." He lauds the film as "a highly exciting tale of stark terror, of high romance, tawdry and home-spun. It is glittery and sordid. It is stimulating with gaiety and with defeat." Not everyone was equally impressed. A contemporary review by Craig Butler called it "an uneven crime drama" and asserted that Steve Fisher's screenplay "starts out promisingly" but continues that its characters are "not developed sufficiently," especially Johnny Kelly and Wally Cassel. Butler adds of Cassel's character that through his Mechanical Man "the sheer strangeness of his job does fascinate." Butler found the dialogue too often "either artificial or bland" and believed the plot "eventually becomes overly busy." Still, he said when director John H. Auer's direction "hits, he really hits hard," singling out a Mechanical Man scene as nothing short of "magical" and praising a chase sequence as "spectacular." He also found John L. Russell's cinematography "electric" and called it "an orgy of high contrast and deep focuses that is stunning." A contemporary *Variety* review wrote, "Production and direction loses itself occasionally in stretching for mood and nuances." Unlike Butler, the *Variety* staff was hardly awed by Russell's cinematography, writing that it "makes okay use of Chicago streets and buildings for the low-key, night-life effect required to back the melodrama." Writing about the previously mentioned Martin Scorsese retrospective on Republic Pictures for *The Village Voice*, Farran Smith Nehme comments that Wally Cassell's "Mechanical Man" makes the greatest impression of all characters in the film: "The degradation of this all-night commercial charade is where *City That Never Sleeps* briefly shades into something close to horror."

In her role as Lydia, the hash slinger turned upper-class housewife turned deceitful adulteress who not only double crosses her husband but also double crosses her lover, Marie hits every note with perfection: affectionate, sensuous, betrayed, bitter, joyful, ashamed, and terrified as Lydia's wild ride requires.

So This Is Love is a misleading title as the motion picture is not a romance but a light-hearted biopic of early 20th century singer Grace Moore. It is also called *The Grace Moore Story*—a far more fitting title. Written by John Monks Jr. and directed by Gordon Douglas, *So This Is Love* is filmed in glorious Technicolor. It stars Kathryn Grayson as Grace Moore and Merv Griffin as her suitor Buddy Nash. Then-child actress Noreen Corcoran puts in an unforgettable performance as Grace Moore when a feisty child. She is feisty indeed as we first meet her riding an elephant as her outraged Daddy, Colonel James Moore (Walter Abel) takes her down from the creature. Through its brightly colored settings and clothing, the Technicolor flick is a treat for the eyes. Through its lovely soprano singing, it is a treat for the ears. However, its script is not particularly outstanding. A contemporary *New York Times* review called it a "pleasing, if uninspired, musical biography" and noted that it is "handsomely tinted in varied hues of Technicolor." The review said it is "more effective musically than it is as a depiction of a colorful success story." This writer believes part of what makes the title inappropriate is that our heroine ultimately chooses career over romance. Alas, our busy Marie Windsor has only a single scene as Marilyn Montgomery, an actress who gets sick so understudy Grace Moore can take her part. Marie's walk-on is chiefly memorable for the remarkably wide hat on her head!

The Eddie Cantor Story is another biopic released in 1953 in which Marie played. Although both biographies and biographical films tend to be made of figures who are deceased—with some observers believing it inappropriate to write biographies of people who are still alive—Eddie Cantor was alive, albeit it past his prime, in 1953. Thus, the real Cantor appears early in the film, arriving at a studio for a private screening of *The Eddie Cantor Story* with his wife Ida. Just prior to the rolling of the film, Cantor whispers to his dearest, "Ida, I've never been so nervous in all my life." The story starts in 1904 on the economically depressed East Side neighborhood of New York City. Young Eddie, 13, craves acceptance of neighborhood hoodlum Rocky Kramer. Eddie happily entertains a crowd with his singing. Unbeknownst to our young hero, Rocky and his crew use the distraction to pick audience members' pockets. Realizing what is going on, a police officer takes Eddie home to his Grandma Esther. Then, carrying Sabbath candles, our young Eddie head to the home of David

Tobias, a local businessperson. There, daughter Ida Tobias invited Eddie to stay for dinner (ah! Young love buds and blooms!). Not long after, we see our Eddie at a camp where his singing goes over big. The youthful singer wins a theater contest, then the eye—and ear—of a producer who leads Eddie into a cabaret. He travels with the show. Reaching adulthood, he heads back home where he learns Rocky Kramer is now a corrupt politician in league with Tammany Hall. But Rocky offers Eddie a job as a singer waiter at a Coney Island nightclub which Eddie accepts. To impress Ida and her family, Eddie claims to be the star of the nightclub's shows. The truth is discovered with the Tobias family visits. Ida is disillusioned and disappointed. Her unhappiness disappears when Eddie tells her that a producers wants him to perform in London—and he proposes marriage to Ida. The couple wed. Then Eddie discovers the producer is unable to come through. However, famous comedian Jimmy Durante gets Eddie a position with a Los Angeles, California show called *Canary Cottage.*

It is in the *Canary Cottage* segment that Marie first makes an appearance in this movie. She plays star Cleo Abbott who turns green with envy when Eddie draws audience attention away from her. She comes up with a sly plan to rid herself of this scene stealer. Cleo informs Eddie that legendary theater producer Florenz Ziegfeld wants Eddie in his *Follies.* Overjoyed, Eddie scurries back to the Big Apple—only to learn that Ziegfeld does not even know who he is! But Eddie, desperate to further his career as well as support his wife and their new baby, talks the producer into letting Eddie try out in that evening's show. He sings *How Ya' Gonna Keep 'Em Down on the Farm After They've Seen Paree*—and is an overnight sensation! The movie continues to tell the story of this brilliant entertainer. At the close of the movie, the audience sees the real Eddie and Ida back in the projection film.

14 Small Screen, Big Screen, Nuptials For Keeps

EARLY IN 1954, on January 23, the kick-off episode of the television series *Stories of the Century*, an episode in which Marie guest starred, was broadcast. This series was set in the Old West and followed the adventures of railroad detective Matt Clark (Jim Davis) who tracks down bandits victimizing the railroad.

The kick-off episode was "Belle Starr" and Marie played the title character. A "user reviewer" on the Internet Movie Database (IMDb) "thought it a bit curious that the producers of *Stories of the Century* would lead off with [an episode] about a woman" considering "all the famous [male] outlaws whose names became household words." In this writer's opinion, the producers probably thought focusing on a rare female Old West outlaw would lend this initial episode a special flavor.

And indeed it did. Marie's standard rootin' tootin' cowboy drag is dramatically set off with a hat that flaunts a flamboyant white feather.

The story opens on a quasi-humorous note as Belle Star rides her horse to a saloon where she chastises her husband Sam (Ric Roman) for blowing their money on a card game. She reminds him that he was supposed to put their money in the bank and derides him as a "shiftless bum!" Pointing her gun at his card game partners, Belle scoops the lost loot back into her hat.

Matt Clark is hot on Belle's trail as she and her gang recently rustled a herd of horses. He is aided by law enforcement agent Frankie Adams (Mary Castle) who, posing as a dressmaker, has pulled the infamous Belle Starr into a web. Frankie tells us that, for all her banditry, Belle is still a woman and, like most women, relishes a pretty dress.

Part of what spices the episode is Belle's competency in the "man's world" of the outlaw but her insistence on her femininity as when she tells her husband, "Don't you know how to treat a lady? Open the door!" Another time she shouts, "Hats off in the presence of ladies!"

The quickly moving half hour is filled with a lot of shooting plus a catfight between Belle and Frankie. Justice triumphs in the end. In the coda we are informed that Belle and husband Sam served a year behind bars for their horse stealing. Released from jail, they returned to their criminal ways. Matt is historically accurate when he notes that Belle Starr was murdered with the identity of the murderer remaining a mystery. The previously quoted reviewer asserted that Marie was "not the least bit subtle in her characterization of the female horse thief and all around bad girl." The reviewer is accurate as this role did not call for subtlety but for the flamboyance Marie gave it. Another IMDb reviewer notes Marie's abilities on a horse made her an actress "born to play Belle Star" and "wishes she had done so in a feature." He praises both Jim Davis and Marie for their "fine horsemanship." In *Ladies of the Western: Interviews with Fifty-One More Actresses from the Silent Era to the Television Westerns of the 1950s and 1960s*, authors Michael G. Fitzgerald and Boyd Magers report that the Belle Starr role in this TV show was "one of [Marie's] favorite" television roles.

Marie appeared on the small screen in 1954 on *Pantomime Quiz*, a game show based on the parlor game of charades. The TV show had two teams of four contestants each. In the rounds, one team member mimed a name or phrase and the other three tried to guess it. The team that took the least time to guess all the phrases/names won the game. When introducing guest panelist Marie Windsor, host Mike Stokey described her as a "popular actress and sportswoman." Others on the show were such regular panelists as Fred Clark, Adele Jergens, Jackie Coogan, Frank De Vol, Fritz Feld, Glenn Langan, and Paul Cavanaugh. The episode Marie appeared on featured no names but only phrases which were displayed to the TV audience by assistant Sandra Spence who, at one point, invited audience members to send in suggestions to "stump the stars." Several phrases chosen would not be shown today as they are rife with sexism, ableism, ethnocentrism, and even racism.

The phrase that Marie mimed was "A whistling girl and a crowing hen never come to any good end." The phrase suggests females must never step outside gender roles—a suggestion not just "politically incorrect" but, in this writer's opinion, quite offensive. There is also a whiff of irony as Marie often played women unafraid to defy gender stereotypes.

Another awful phrase mimed in this episode was "Her lower lip was round and full—too full. She was a Ubangi." A Ubangi is a female in an area of Chad in which it is customary for females to distend their lower lips with wooden disks. The description of the lower lip as "too full" is, of course, based on the ethnocentric Western prejudice that non-Western standards of beauty are inferior. Still another: "A Hottentot taught a Hottentot tot." The last phrase may not actually be racist but it could well be viewed as insensitive in today's world in the way it plays on the word for an ethnic group.

An element of prejudice against little people can be seen in the phrase, "The death of two midgets or two short biers." "Midgets" is a term considered pejorative by Little People/Dwarves. To be fair, there were also quite neutral phrases mimed such as "The monkey married the baboon's sister, smacked his lips and then he kissed her" and "A fat purse makes a soft pillow."

Marie acquitted herself well on the show. She did energetic and creative miming and guessed her share of words—although her team ultimately lost.

"Fatal Fraud" was the title of a 1954 episode of *The Whistler* television series in which Marie appeared. In this episode, Marie played an ambiguous character named Katherine. *The Whistler* was based on the Old Time Radio show of the same name. Like the radio show, the TV series always began with the sound of a man whistling and a narrator describing a situation. "Fatal Fraud" is set in Hong Kong among expatriates from the West. It starts at a small dinner party at the home of wealthy Van Loovan (John Banner). Comedian Chris Moore (Patric Knowles) is performing. He shows off his impressive ability to imitate varied voices and accents. Among those admiring him is Marie's character Katherine who joins the others in heartily applauding Chris. The party ends. We get an idea of Chris's circumstances when he asks one of the partiers, Binkers (Pat Aherne) for a loan. We get an even better idea of the plight Chris is in when he returns to the hotel at which he has been staying. The hotel clerk (Stanley Farrar) says he cannot get back into his room unless he coughs up his overdue fee. He is aghast at the possibility of being locked out of his room but before things can get too bad, Katherine appears. She pays his fee and invites him to a better place where he need not pay.

Katherine soon makes it clear that she needs the performer's unique vocal talents for a scheme to bilk her employer, Van Loovan, out of a quarter of a million dollars' worth of goods scheduled to be transported by plane. The plan is for Chris to imitate Van Loovan and direct the plane to land elsewhere. The loot will be divided between Katherine, Chris, and radio operator-conspirator Rene Simmoneau (John Berardino). Katherine sweetens an already sweet deal by leading Chris to believe she is sweet on him! As an IMDb reviewer observes, "What guy would say no to the cash as well as the charms of Miss Windsor." Events lead Chris to wonder about Katherine's supposed affection for him: Is it real or is she feigning it to get his services? A crisis is precipitated when Chris picks up a note indicating Katherine is planning a double cross. But he is uncertain *who* she wants to double cross. Does she want to cut Rene out so the two of them can divide the goods in half instead of three ways? Or is it Chris who she wants to unload so she can run off with Rene? And just *how* can Chris discover her true intentions? These questions are answered in a startling and violent climax. As the previously quoted IMDb writer elaborated, Marie "makes this one look easy as she does her bit."

1954 was an important year for Marie Windsor on the personal front. As previously mentioned, Marie's dedication to her career did not mean she lacked for non-work related interests. In August 1954, actor William Bakewell arranged for her to go on a blind date with real estate agent Jack Hupp. Luckily for both of them, Jack Hupp was not unfamiliar with the entertainment industry as he was the son of silent film actor and screenwriter Earle Rodney. Perhaps his family background meant that he understood Marie and enjoyed discussing her work with her. Perhaps Marie's love of sports made the athletic Jack Hupp—he had been on the 1936 Olympic basketball team and would eventually be inducted into the USC Athletic Hall of Fame—especially attractive to her. At any rate, it is a certainty the attraction was powerful and that it deepened into genuine affection: the wedding of Jack Hupp and Marie Windsor took place in November 1954.

Unlike the brief marriage Marie had previously, this one proved the real thing, lasting until death did them part. When Marie became a wife for the second time, she also became stepmother to Chris Hupp, Jack's son from a previous union.

Hell's Half Acre, a black and white film noir in which Marie had a supporting role, was released in 1954. It may well be the only film noir set in Hawaii and was certainly the first set there. Unfortunately, the black and white filming did not do cinematic justice to the lush setting. Still, *Hell's Half Acre* is an interesting crime drama and benefits from its rather unusual setting. Steve Fisher wrote the screenplay for it and John

H. Auer directed it. The credits cite "Don the Beachcomber" as "technical adviser."

At the start of the flick, we are at a banquet in Hawaii. A woman is placing leis over Sally Lee (Nancy Gates) and Chet Chester (Wendell Corey). Entertainment includes a song called *Polynesian Rhapsody* which was apparently crafted by our Mr. Chester. A note is slipped to the table shared by Sally and Chet. Sally reads the note and heads to another room to meet its author. The fellow is a criminal who was once in cahoots with Chet and now wants hush money. To protect her boyfriend, beautiful Sally coldly murders the blackmailer. She reveals the murder to Chet who insists on taking the blame for it. The couple agree that he will confess to the killing but claim that the murder occurred accidentally in a struggle over the gun.

Cut to the mainland. Donna Williams (Evelyn Keyes) realizes that a lovely record, *Polynesian Rhapsody*, has a line identical to one left in a note by her husband Randy Williams. It has long been assumed that Randy perished in the Japanese attack on Pearl Harbor, leaving not only a widow behind, but the child of his that she bore in his absence. Randy's son is now eleven and Donna is engaged to a man named Frank (Robert Shield). However, she has long suspected that Randy was not killed and might still be alive. She hands Frank his engagement ring: "I can't be engaged to you if my husband is still alive." Then she heads to Hawaii.

In the meantime, authorities take Chet to the morgue to identify a body—the body of Sally Lee. Wily Chet manages to escape his captors and, in the manner of film heroes, seeks to do his own investigation to bring to justice the murderer of his murdered girlfriend (who happened to also be a murderer).

When Donna sees a picture of Chet, she thinks he is probably Randy but is unsure as Chet has a facial scar Randy did not have. Believing a man escaped from police custody would take refuge in Honolulu's unsavory district called "Hell's Half Acre," Donna goes there and gets a job as a taxi dancer. Ne'er do well Ippy (Leonard Strong) informs Chet of the taxi dancer who says she is related to him and is searching for him.

Adding to the brew is the shadowy Roger Kong (Philip Ahn) an underworld figure who, like the cops and Donna, is searching for Chester.

The film is about halfway over before Marie makes an appearance. Marie's character is the loud and rather obnoxious Rose. We see Rose working in a kitchen. She hears Tubby Otis (Jesse White) snoring and walks into the room. Tubby is sharing a room but not a bed with Donna.

"You were in pretty bad shape last night," Rose informs Donna. Then she splashes water on the snoring Tubby, telling him, "Go on, you've slept long enough." Donna is confused and Rose admits she is married to "that," meaning Tubby. Hubby brought the woman there because she had passed out.

Who should arrive but Roger Kong who apparently pays Tubby for varied dirty jobs. Whereas Marie played a white woman who objected to an interracial marriage between a white man and an Asian woman in *Japanese War Bride*, in this film she plays a white woman adulterously in love with the Asian Roger Kong. Her impatience with Tubby contrasts sharply to her romantic warmth for Roger Kong.

Events soon bring Chet and Donna together. Donna is sure he is Randy although he denies it—even after being informed of a child. Is it really a case of mistaken identity? Could Chet be Randy with amnesia? Does he just want to escape from his responsibilities? Is he ashamed of something he did in the past?

After some more adventures and tensions, the answers will gradually appear. Rose will be seen in a few more scenes: nonchalantly smoking as her lover brutally pummels her husband, equally nonchalant as she turns up the radio to disguise the noises made during a murder, dancing coolly at a nightclub, and drunkenly celebrating her status as a widow.

Hell's Half Acre was reviewed in *The New York Times* where the writer stated that "there are moments it's downright exciting" and that "betwixt the start and the finish, an undemanding spectator will find enough sequences of merit to hold his interest." The reviewer praised Evelyn Keyes as "a luscious young thing who certainly earns her 'A' in acting." The reviewer praised Fisher's "economical script" and Auer's direction as "one of sensible brevity without unnecessary frills."

Another Marie vehicle hitting the big screen in 1954 was *The Bounty Hunter*. Filmed in "WarnerColor," the flick had a screenplay by Winston Miller and was directed by André De Toth. *The Bounty Hunter* is a Western starring Randolph Scott and was the sixth and last Western starring Scott that De Toth directed. It is also believed to be the first Western in which a bounty hunter is its hero.

There is a brief onscreen written paragraph explaining what a bounty hunter does. Soon we see bounty hunter Jim Kipp (Scott) skillfully outwit and outgun a wanted man who tries unsuccessfully to ambush him. Kipp takes the suspect's dead body into town. There a representative of the Pinkerton Detective Agency requests that Kipp, who is famed for his smarts as well as his quick-on-the-draw talents, try to find a trio of masked robbers who perpetrated a holdup that netted them $100,000. There is a hefty reward and the task is well suited to Kipp who readily accepts it.

Our hero rides his horse into Twin Folks where he uses the alias "Collins." Knowing that one of the trio he hunts got a leg shot in the robbery, Kipp seeks information from the Twin Folks sawbones, Dr. Spencer (Harry Antrim). The good doc acknowledges treating someone for a gunshot in the leg around the time of the robbery but holds more information close to his chest. With Dr. Spencer is his lovely daughter, Julie Spencer (Dolores Dorn) who is perplexed by her Dad's reluctance to be more forthcoming. Kipp is immediately attracted to Julie.

In another scene, Kipp questions hotel employee Bill Rachin (Ernest Borgnine)—a man who walks with a limp. Kipp also wonders about card dealer George Williams (Robert Keys). Borgnine's appearance meant that he often played crude characters, but Marie said of him, "I sure like that man—he's a good actor, too!"

Marie plays the card dealer's wife, Alice Williams. We first see Alice when Kipp moseys into the casino. She is glamorously decked out in a fancy shiny dress with her dark hair up. A fellow harasses her and she slaps the malefactor, yelling, "Let go of me you big ape!" Calmed down, she approaches Kipp at the bar, takes a drink, and toasts a boisterous, "Welcome stranger!" Later in the film she will hold a conversation with him in which she flirts and suggests she might "help" him in his search.

As it turns out, she will play a most surprising role when the story reaches its violent (this is a Western) and quite startling climax. A review of *The Bounty Hunter* in *The Bridgeport Telegram* of Bridgeport, Connecticut states that the picture "depicts a little-known but exciting chapter of early Western frontier life." The piece continues that Dorn and Marie "engage in a ferocious bit of feminine fisticuffs" that is "one of the most fiercely fought screen imbroglios ever seen between two girls [still in the era when women were "girls" in old age] on the screen."

Marie got first billing in the 1955 crime drama *No Man's Woman*. To modern people, the title may suggest women's independence and empowerment. It might even suggest lesbianism or celibacy. However, this film was made decades prior to the second wave of the women's movement and had nothing to do with such issues. Rather, the protagonist Marie plays, anti-heroine Carolyn Ellenson Grant, is a woman who is interested in *too many men* to be any particular man's woman.

No Man's Woman had a screenplay by John K. Butler and was directed by Franklin Adreon. It is structured much like an episode of the old *Perry Mason* TV show. Carolyn is shown interacting with a variety of people and gives each of them a reason to want her dead. When she is murdered midway through the film, there is no courtroom scene or confession but there is a search to see which of our possible murderers did the dirty deed.

The movie opens with a convertible, the top of it down, driving on a highway. A large painting ubiquitously takes up much of the backseat and the paper wrapping it is being blown by the wind. The driver of the vehicle, Carolyn, stops the car and asks Wayne Vincent (Patric Knowles) to do something about the paper. He rips it off and tosses it out of the vehicle (this pre-dated concerns with littering). He would like to take this opportunity for some necking with lovely Carolyn but she nixes it as she has been invited to talk with someone. "I must show him some consideration," she relates. "After all he is my husband." Later in the film we learn that Carolyn and Wayne are secretly an "item" while publicly Wayne, an art critic, devotes his column to admiring the work in her art gallery.

Cut to estranged hubby Harlow Grant (John Archer) and his ladylove Louise Nelson (Nancy Gates). Louise scoots into another room so Harlow and Carolyn may speak privately. Harlow is anxious to divorce Carolyn so he can wed Louise. Carolyn is happy receiving alimony and sees no reason to completely cut their connection. Harlow presses and she says she would be willing to divorce Harlow providing he gives her an *extremely* generous divorce settlement. He says he would have to sell too much of his firm and Carolyn suggests selling his father's interest in it as "he's getting old and it's time the old buzzard retired anyhow." He knocks a glass out of her hand—and she raises the demand.

Out comes Louise together with Harlow's Dad, Phillip Grant (Douglas Wood). Dad offers to increase the money Carolyn gets in a divorce. Nothing doing and Carolyn sashays away. As the trio she leaves commiserate, Phillip remarks, "Any way you look at it, that woman's a witch." "And any way you spell it," Harlow answers, skirting the anti-profanity words censorship of the day.

Carolyn is the proud owner of an art gallery. She employs pretty and perky Betty Allen (Jil Jarmyn) as assistant. Carolyn knows that Betty expects her fiancé so Carolyn ensures Betty is not around when the fellow shows up. Carolyn wants to check him out. He turns out to be handsome Dick Sawyer (Richard Crane) to whom our Carolyn is immediately attracted. A few scenes pass and Carolyn leaves Betty in charge of the art gallery with an excuse about urgently needing to "scout paintings with Mr. Vincent."

The true mission Carolyn does is to spend time with Dick on his boat. She poses as having an intense interest in fishing and basically invites herself aboard so she can spend time with the handsome fellow who has caught her eye.

In the meantime, who should show up at the Carolyn Grant Art Gallery but Wayne Vincent? Wayne and Betty think Carolyn must have gotten her dates confused. Wayne agrees to watch the gallery and Betty heads to the fishing wharf to meet Dick. She learns he is on his boat with another lady.

When the boat docks, Carolyn suggests the two of them attend a formal dinner dance. Dick balks. After all, he *is* engaged. "I gave a ring to a gal named Betty Allen," he asserts. "And I gave it to her for keeps." Wily Carolyn threatens to inform Betty of their boat trip but make it seem like it was his idea and quite sordid. Carolyn's lack of scruples baffles Dick who is astonished that anyone would try to blackmail him into a date. "Carolyn, I spent six years in the merchant marines," he tells her. "I ran into an awful lot of no-good woman in just about every part of the world but I never once went into one like you!" She slaps his face and drives off.

At her art gallery, Carolyn is startled to find Wayne Vincent instead of Betty. Wayne informs her that Betty is quitting her job. Then, suspecting the tale she told Betty about wanting to look at paintings in his company was not simple confusion but a subterfuge, he inquires as to her whereabouts that day. She refuses to answer. Then she learns that superiors at his newspaper discovered his financial and personal interest in the Carolyn Grant Art Gallery. He has lost his job—and been blacklisted from the entire field of art criticism. Wayne expresses dismay at his smashed future but tries to cheer himself up with "we still have each other." Carolyn sets him straight: if he cannot promote her art gallery, he is history. She shows the disappointed suitor the door.

Louise knocks on the door. She briefly pleads with Carolyn to make an appropriate settlement with Harlow and is also told to leave.

There is an intense scene between Dick Sawyer and Betty Allen. Dick insists that he has zero interest in Carolyn and she "is not worth us breaking up." Betty believes what Carolyn said in a recent call that Dick wanted Carolyn on that boat. Betty tells Dick off and he insists that the only reason he would want to see Carolyn is to "push her off the boat right in the middle of the Pacific Ocean."

Carolyn is restlessly sleeping when a noise disturbs her. She gets up and smokes a cigarette (huh?) before investigating. Then someone unseen by the audience shoots and kills conniving Carolyn.

The set-up is that we have no less than six folks who have good reason to want Carolyn Grant out of the way: Harlow Grant, Louise Nelson, Philip Grant, Betty Allen, Dick Sawyer, and Wayne Vincent.

So who did the dirty deed? The rest of the flick is spent ferreting out the murderer.

Marie's playing of Carolyn Grant is not nuanced because the script does not call for it. Rather, Marie gives the audience a character we-love-to-hate who never fails to sparkle with vivacious villainy. Film critic John Nail observes that in every scene she appears, we see "Windsor stealing the show as the happily remorseless Carolyn." Another movie reviewer, Martin Teller, writes, "All the best stuff is Windsor being awful and manipulative." However, the movie is a "ho-hum whodunit" and it "dries up once Carolyn is out of the picture." On the website *Laura's Miscellaneous Musings*, Laura (no last name given), states: "The fun is in watching a group of familiar actors doing their thing, starting with the flamboyantly naughty Marie Windsor, who seems to be having the time of her life doing everybody wrong."

No Man's Woman is sometimes called a "film noir" but its scenes are not dark enough—in the literal sense—to be a true noir. Indeed, most scenes are drenched in either sunlight or Edison-legacy light. It is more of a crime procedural film. It has no artistic aspirations or depth but it is entertaining, albeit not particularly memorable.

Marie played in a much more light-hearted flick that was also released in 1955 and in which she starred with one of the most famous comedy duos in history: *Abbott and Costello Meet the Mummy*.

Abbott and Costello had started in vaudeville and followed the common line from stage to radio to film. They made a series of motion pictures—most with Universal and all of them hits with the public—in which their routines were seen in varied settings like the Army or Navy, in high society or college, or in locations ranging from Africa to Hollywood to Alaska to Mexico to the Old West to Venus (the latter in a film oddly titled *Abbott and Costello Go to Mars* although their true destination was Venus that was filled with beautiful Venusian women without menfolk, reminiscent of Marie's movie about the moon). In 1948, the duo commenced a series of motion picture comedies in which they encountered various classic monsters like Dracula, Frankenstein's creation (who is usually called "Frankenstein" after creator Dr. Victor Frankenstein), the Invisible Man—and, in 1955, a mummy.

Abbott and Costello Meet the Mummy begins with our heroes in Cairo, Egypt. The dynamic duo overhear Dr. Gustav Zoomer (Kurt Katch) talk about a mummy named Klaris (Edwin Parker) who is the guardian of the Tomb of Princess Ara from Ancient Egypt. The mummy also possesses a sacred but—wouldn't you know it?—cursed medallion that shows where Princess Ara, and the treasures buried with her, can be found. Also overhearing the conversation with this all-important information are cult leader Semu (Richard Deacon) and the scheming Madame Rontru whom Marie plays. Madame Rontru is a businessperson who is determined to get her hands on the treasures of Princess Ara. The greedy Madame Rontru badly wants that medallion that she believes will lead her to the treasures. When Madame Rontru is reminded that there is a curse on the medallion, she retorts, "There is no curse that a gun or a knife can't cure!" After battling the mummy with a gun, then a torch, and finally a stick of dynamite, she is warned by an associate, "He's dangerous!" Her ready reply, "So am I!"

Seeking a job that will take them back to America, Abbott and Costello go to Dr. Zoomer's for a position guarding the mummy that Dr. Z plans to ship to the United States. However, before our heroes arrive, two minions of Semu, Hetsut (Richard Karian) and Iben (Mel Welles) have spirited Klaris away. But they did not take the medallion! Abbott and Costello take that. They try to sell it to Madame Rontru. Abbott insists on a price of $5,000. She does not have the money on her. They agree to meet at the Cairo Café and complete the deal. It is at this eatery that the pair learn from a frightened waiter that the medallion is cursed. This leads to a broadly comic scene which ends with Costello *swallowing* the medallion! When Rontru arrives and learns the odd placement of what she seeks, she takes Lou Costello to a doctor who does an X-ray. Sure enough, the medallion shows up. A series of often slapstick style shenanigans follow. All the protagonists—Abbott and Costello, Rontru, Semu—meet the mummy who has, of course (this is a movie) come back to life.

How did Marie feel about working with Abbott and Costello? She found them "both terrific to work with." She added that she had heard that the pair were "not getting on too well" at the time but that could have just been unfounded gossip as she "wasn't aware of it" from what she saw of them. "On the set and in their scenes they seemed to be comfortable with each other," she stated. "They did ad-lib a lot when they did their scenes together, but if they had dialogue with other actors, they stuck to the script pretty much." She added that Costello was more apt that his partner to "kid around and chitchat on the set."

The film is quite entertaining and was, like most work from Abbott and Costello, well-received by the public. On July 20, 1955, the Casper, Wyoming newspaper *Casper Star-Tribune* ran a headline praising the movie as "hilarious." *The Bristol Herald Courier* of Bristol, Tennessee called *Abbott and Costello Meet the Mummy* "side-splitting." A review published on October 4, 1955 in a Staunton, Virginia newspaper *The Daily News Leader*, praised the film as representing "two milestones in the history of the popular comedians." It continued, "First their new film offering is a milestone in the field of mirth. Secondly it represents a milestone in the fact that it is their fortieth film together—and judging from yesterday's audience—it is their best to date."

Although Marie had already demonstrated her comedy chops in other films, movie commentator Rob Nixon observed, "Windsor enjoyed doing comedy and was given many timing tips by Costello during shooting of the picture." Any tips the distinguished comic gave her must have been put to good use as her timing is superb in this film. Laura Wagner commented that Marie "plays it straight and wicked as Madame Rontru, oozing pure evil—every inch the Egyptian villainess."

Abbott and Costello Meet the Mummy turned out to be the final motion picture in the horror-comedy series that the legendary comedians had filmed. It was also their last movie for Universal Studios. They would make only one more film together, *Dance with Me, Henry* (1956). Their partnership drew to a close as Costello suffered increasing health problems prior to his death in 1959 of a heart attack.

1955 also saw the release of a Western in which Marie starred, *The Silver Star*. The screenplay was written by Richard Bartlett and Ian Mac-Donald who also authored the original story. Bartlett directed the movie. Set in the late 1880s, *The Silver Star* begins with Sheriff Bill Dowdy (Edgar Buchanan) retired from the office in the town of Boyce. Dowdy urges friend Gregg Leech (Earle Lyon) to run for sheriff. Reluctant to do so, Leech allows himself to be talked into it. He runs against lawyer John W. Harmon (Lon Chaney Jr.) and easily wins. Marie plays Gregg's fiancée Karen Childress. At a victory rally, she inquires why he was so reluctant to take on the office of sheriff. Gregg tells her he comes from a line of sheriffs as both his Dad and Grandfather held that office—and both were killed in the line of duty. Gregg fears that being a sheriff will interfere with his duties as a husband and (presumably at some point) father. Karen does her best to assure him that she is confident he can be both sheriff and family man. She is proud of the victory of the man she is engaged to marry and places a victory banner in front of the Boyce Hotel.

However, Gregg finds an internal conflict as duty leads him to arrest his close friend, Ward Blythe, for refusing to obey orders about not taking a gun into Boyce.

Gregg's horse starts limping and requires help so Gregg takes the equine to blacksmith Henry "Tiny" Longtree (Barton MacLane). The blacksmith says he voted for Harmon because he does not believe Gregg has what it takes to keep law and order in the town. While they have this uncomfortable conversation, three fellow ride into town, well-known gunman King Daniels (Richard Bartlett) and two associates. They rip down the banner celebrating Gregg's victory. A man named Bainey (Steve Rowland) tries to prevent them from taking down the banner and they assault him.

The terrible trio saunter into the saloon owned by Karen's Dad, Charlie Childress (Morris Ankrum). A distressed Karen asks that they return the banner and King Daniels nonchalantly informs her that he plans to kill Gregg Leech. All this leads to an ultimate showdown. Does Gregg have what it takes to keep peace in Boyce? Will he disappoint Karen or make her proud? Needless to say, the questions are answered before credits roll.

Reviewer Mark Franklin calls *The Silver Star* an "interesting variant on the *High Noon* theme that might have been special with the right director and cast." Franklin continues that Bartlett was not the right director so the resulting picture "lacks the rising tension it needed to make it a success." He also faults Earle Lyon for a "most uninspired performance." Reviewer Stuart Galbraith IV says that "despite the presence of such B-movie favorites as John Agar, Lon Chaney Jr., Edgar Buchanan, and Marie Windsor," the movie is "a pretty feeble offering for die-hard Western fans only."

Discussing *The Silver Star*, Marie commented that more than one person had asked whether she had seen Lon Chaney Jr. either drinking on-set or seeming to be drunk. She said she never saw any evidence of his inebriation during filming. "I didn't get to know Lon very well because the movie had a short schedule and we didn't have a lot of scenes to do together," she said. "As far as I was concerned, he was a very nice man who had a good sense of humor."

Another Western released in 1955 did not have Marie in a starring role but supporting part. Norman Jolley and Richard Bartlett co-authored a screenplay based on a story Jolley wrote. Barlett directed it. *Two-Gun Lady* saw Peggie Castle star as trick-shot artist Kate Masters. Although it is unlikely the filmmakers had any social or political goals in making the movie, *Two-Gun Lady* has what can be seen as feminist implications. Close to its opening, two little boys are roughhousing and poo-pooing the possibility of a woman being skilled with guns. "No one can beat my dad at shooting, much less some *girl*," one of the children declares. But we soon find that Kate Masters has a skill not usually acquired by members of her sex in those days. Accompanied by her manager, Doc McGinnis (Joe Besser), the performer breezes into the town to do her act at Big Mike Dougherty's (Robert Lowery) saloon.

Although the talented trick-shot artist usually performs her act in big cities, she earlier wrote a letter to Mike asking that she do her thing at his business. As much as Big Mike likes the patronage she is sure to draw (no pun intended), he cannot help but be puzzled that she wants to do her act in such a small and humble town. It occurs to him that she and Doc could be law enforcement people investigating his checkered past. Then a stranger, Dan Corbin (William Talman), happens into the town. Dan finds his way to the Ivers ranch where he has an enlightening conversation with teenager Jenny Ivers (Barbara Turner). She explains that her Dad can no longer do gun battles because his arm was paralyzed in one but that he likes to provoke other people into such dangerous confrontations. Dan also learns that, on this cattle ranch, Jenny has a pet lamb that she loves and cherishes. Dan also finds himself strongly attracted to Kate and there are signs this is a returned attraction.

Cut to Mike's saloon where Jenny's elder brother, Ben Ivers (Earle Lyon), returns after pulling off a bank robbery. He is there to meet with the character Marie plays, a saloon hostess named Bess who pretends to be in love with Mike although she pines for Ben. After some passionate kissing, Ben informs his girlfriend that he will lay low for a period to throw lawmen off his scent. Then he will fetch Bess and the two will live happily ever after on his ill-gotten gains.

That evening's show has Kate doing her act for a big crowd. She is able to shoot pieces of chalk out of people's hands even when she has her back turned and must do her measuring by looking in a mirror. Naturally, people are very impressed by this display. It seems that a mere "girl" can be a good shooter after all!

While Kate astounds the audience with her skill, Bess tries to get an increasingly drunken Doc to spill the beans on why the pair of them came into such humble environs to show off Kate's tricks. When Doc and Kate meet after her show, Kate wants to know what Doc said to Bess. He does not know because alcohol fogged his memory.

Eventually it comes out that there is a very special reason the famous Kate Masters has come to this little cowtown: Kate Masters is really Karen Marshall, daughter of a mother and father who were brutally gunned down by the Ivers men in a property dispute. She was but a child when she witnessed this horror. As she grew up, she concentrated on learning all she could about guns, not just to put on an entertaining show, but to be equipped to seek vengeance when the time came—and she believes that time has come. Naturally enough, the rest of the film works out whether or not she will find peace from her seething psychic wounds.

Two-Gun Lady is no masterpiece but it is an entertaining flick. A website called "Laura's Miscellaneous Musings" remarks, "I think most 'B' Western movie fans would agree that any Western starring *both* Peggie Castle and Marie Windsor is a must-see." She continued that the movie is "71 minutes of enjoyable entertainment."

The 1956 *Swamp Women* had Marie once again acting with Jil Jarmyn of *No Man's Woman*. Directed by Roger Corman, often called "The Pope of Pop Cinema," with a screenplay by David Stern, the cheaply made crime/adventure flick also stars beauties Carole Mathews, Susan Cummings, and Beverly Garland. It also stars handsome Mike Connors who would win greatest fame as private detective Joe Mannix in the TV series *Mannix*. *Swamp Women* is a color film which is to its advantage as the audience is apt to enjoy seeing the lush hues of the swamp itself as well as the colors sported by the female characters.

At the start of *Swamp Women*, we see a couple passionately kissing at a Mardi Gras celebration. The couple consists of Bob Matthews (Mike Connors) and Marie (Susan Cummings). The smooch ends and the couple drift through the revelers. Bob is approached by a down-on-his-luck drunk who begs for a bit of help. The caring Bob hands the panhandler a few bucks. However, we soon learn that Bob lost considerably more than he gave away as a cop arrests Charlie the Pickpocket (Jonathan Haze) and takes him into the station. Not only is the fellow a thief rather than a panhandler but he is stone cold sober. Police Lieutenant Lee Hampton (Carole Matthews) points this out after he lifts her wallet—which she, alert cop that she is, immediately lifts back!

Perhaps the above scene is meant to make the point that things are not always what they seem to be. This is an important point as the entire plot of the film involves Policewoman Lee going undercover and pretending to be an imprisoned crook. There is a gang of thieves known as the Nardo Gang. The gang's male members are no more: they all took a trip to the electric chair. However, the gang's female members are imprisoned. The whole bunch was caught after they made a huge haul of diamonds. The gems were not found when the Nardo Gang were and are still missing.

Lee and her superior, a police sergeant (Ed Nelson) whose name is never mentioned, hatch a plan that will allow authorities to recover the stolen goods. Lee will go undercover as an inmate in the prison where the Nardo Gang female members are kept. The authorities will arrange for the women to find an easy way to "escape" the prison and Lee will accompany them to their ill-gotten gains.

The Nardo Gang women consist of Josie Nardo, played by Marie, red-haired and bad-tempered Vera (Beverly Garland), and platinum blonde Billie (Jil Jarmyn). Lee makes friends with them and they agree to cut her in on the loot when she informs them of a way to run to freedom.

That run to freedom soon leads them to a swamp. All four escapees soon cut their clothing so four pairs of shapely legs are on full display, providing a treat for the straight males in the audience.

A boat is needed and the gang commandeers the one in which Bob and Marie are meandering down a river. They also take the couple prisoner. Marie is soon gone. The terrified woman attempts to escape and dives into the water. "She can't swim!" Lee realizes and goes into the lake to try a rescue. The kidnappers unloose Bob so he can do the same. Their efforts come to naught as a hungry alligator has seen an opportunity for a meal.

Most of the film shows four scantily clad beauties and one handsome stud with his hands tied behind his back—a set-up guaranteed to trigger many people's kinks. Male audience members are apt to enjoy the cat-fights. Audience members of both genders may enjoy the sight of lovely women entranced by a handsome man in bondage.

Marie delivers a believable performance as the gang's leader. Less likely to just go off on a temper tantrum than her confederates, she is nonetheless easily identifiable as a callous and greedy psychopath.

There is a lot of conflict between the women as tempers go haywire and there is little honor seen among thieves. The brisk pace, swamp setting, and kinky effects all combine to make *Swamp Women* interesting entertainment. Writing for a Memphis, Tennessee newspaper, *The Commercial Appeal*, shortly after the film was released, Ben S. Parker asserts, "Love-starved women convicts escape into a trackless Louisiana swamp, seeking a fortune in diamonds they had cached there, and taking with them a big, handsome man, securely held captive. Boy, oh, boy!" What did this writer say about kink appeal? Parker further writes that the one male is "in the odd position of standing or sitting quietly by, hands tied, while the girls do all the work and the fighting, of which there is plenty." Parker concludes, "*Swamp Women*, which is a bit better entertainment that it's title or its topic would indicate, was filmed in the lush tropic fastnesses of Louisiana's bayou country, and opens with some deceptively cheery shots of the Mardi Gras in full swing." In this writer's opinion, opening on Mardi Gras makes sense to hook a viewer in as there are few things more colorful. Writing far more recently in 2021 on a website called "B&S About Movies," the blogger states that each of the female stars save Carole Matthews plays "the kind of girl who'd sooner punch you in the jaw than kiss you on the lips and that's exactly why I love them all so much."

It should be mentioned that some critics absolutely despise *Swamp Women*. *Filmfanatic.org* asserts that the film features Roger Corman's "worst signature elements: interminable stock footage filler, brawling females, and an illogical, meandering script. Even at 67 minutes, it goes on far too long, and fails to hold interest." That critic continues, "One of its mildly redeeming qualities is statuesque Marie Windsor, who is always fun to watch." The writer speculates that it was not only men who liked watching the lovely female leads but that *Swamp Women* might have been "a big hit with San Francisco's lesbian underground at the time of its release." Movie critic and political commentator Michael Medved included *Swamp Women* in his 1978 book *The Fifty Worst Films of All Time*. Under the title *Swamp Diamonds*, it was mocked by the television show *Mystery Science Theater 3000* (*MST3K*), a program in which a group of cartoon characters make quips as a film they designate a "bad movie" plays.

In an interview in her senior citizen years, Marie disclosed that it took two weeks to film *Swamp Women*. She was scheduled to work on *The Killing* when Corman made *Swamp Women*. "Kubrick was willing to postpone my starting date" so she could be available for the Corman movie. What's more, "Corman was nice enough to let me go home a couple of days earlier" so she could act in *The Killing*. Marie did not have a high opinion of *Swamp Women*. "God, it's just such a corny picture," she groaned. Filming it provided special challenges, Marie disclosed. "We had such a rough location on it," the actress asserted. "We were treading around in mud up to our waists. It looked like there was only about a foot of water and then you'd step down and just keep on going." The performers were in danger that was all-too-real, she continued. "We saw many poisonous snakes swimming around us and I daresay there were many we didn't see! On dry land, we had to jump off trucks and perform activities usually done by stunt people, of whom there were none in this company."

Marie tended to be favorably impressed by directors—or at least was likely to comment on those she liked—so it might not be surprising that she found Roger Corman "a very nice fellow" and a "pleasant, nice director." She said she "never saw him lose his temper about anything" even though the location shots of *Swamp Women* might excuse such a temper loss.

Co-stars Beverly Garland and Mike Connors impressed Marie on a personal level as she made friends with both of them. "Terrific, darling people," she said of them. She added that for years after the filming of *Swamp Women*, she exchanged Christmas cards with both Garland and Connors.

Swamp Women was exposed to a new audience in 1993 when it was aired on the bad-movie mocking TV show *Mystery Science Theater 3000*. For that *MST3K* episode, it was broadcast under the title *Swamp Diamonds*.

Marie's skillful playing of unfaithful wives, female gun slingers, and alluring psychopaths caused a certain amount of emotional turmoil for her. Unfortunately, some people have trouble separating performers as persons from the roles they play. The fact is that actors often have nothing in common with the characters they depict. Marilyn Monroe and Gracie Allen were very intelligent individuals who, in their differing ways, endearingly played dummies. Jewish, Slavic, and gay actors have played Nazis on the screen and stage. Carroll O'Connor, a lifelong Roman Catholic, shot to fame as anti-Catholic Archie Bunker who was, of course, an all-round bigot routinely spouting prejudice against blacks, Jews, and other ethnicities. Robert Ryan, a political liberal and civil rights activist, played anti-Semites and racists. Ryan said he played characters he found "totally despicable."

It is sad but not completely shocking that some people confused the sensitive and kindly Marie Windsor with some of the villainesses she so perfectly impersonated. That confusion led misguided people to send her Bibles in which they underlined the sins her characters had committed!

These odd "gifts" could be accompanied by letters warning her to repent. Marie was not only disturbed but actually frightened by the tone of some of these letters so she took them to the police.

Knowing herself capable of taking on varied roles, she was also concerned about being typecast in "dragon lady" or "femme fatale" roles. It was not that she disliked playing heavies but she wanted to be considered for virtuous roles as well. She started to wonder if her appearance might be contributing to her typecasting. She later recalled that a director—whom she did not name—said, "You have to turn this way because of the shadow of your nose [that] we're trying to avoid." She started to think her nose worked against her getting more virtuous parts and had cosmetic surgery on her nose. The surgery on her nose did not cause any drastic change in her appearance. "It was mostly just removing a bump on her nose," Rick Hupp said. She sometimes regretted the cosmetic surgery. "Sometimes she would say, 'I should have kept my old nose' and other times she said, 'I'm glad I got a nose job,'" Rick Hupp commented. "She wavered a bit."

Although Marie was understandably troubled by her typecasting, there were certainly times in which she was cast to play nice women. For example, a 1954 episode of *Public Defender* entitled "The Ring" allowed Marie to play a kind and moral character as well as bring her powerful real-life maternal instincts into her acting. Marie played carnival performer Melody Scanlon who has been arrested for stealing an expensive ring. Although the ring had been given to her as an engagement ring by suitor Preston Carstairs (Peter Adams) but it turns out that it was not really his to give as it still belongs to his mother (Isabel Randolph). Since Melody is unable to find the ring, mother Carstairs is certain she stole it. This episode takes us into the world of the "carnies" who cherish their nomadic way of life and its contrast with that of the settled "towners" and "natives" as they call those who do not work carnivals. There is a Romeo and Juliet element in the romance between Preston and Melody as her fellow carnies regard it as a kind of betrayal for her to adopt a settled lifestyle and the upper-class Mom Carstairs tells Melody that friends of the snooty Carstairs family would always see Melody as "the girl who danced in a carnival."

Marie's performance as Melody is sympathetic and dignified when she asserts to the frowning elder Carstairs that carnival people are "as nice and as fine and as decent" as any other group of people. There is a strong sense of conviction when she makes this statement that may reflect that feeling of a woman who perfectly impersonated the nasty and the decadent although she was "as nice and as fine and as decent" as could be.

The relationship between Melody and her small daughter Kiki (Jeri Lou James) is pivotal to the episode and Marie is utterly natural in portraying Melody's strong maternal instincts. With little Kiki, Marie portrays a softness of affect, a warmth, and a sense of protectiveness that lends this episode a special charm and poignancy.

1954 saw a significant change in Marie's personal life. She married realtor Jack Rodney Hupp. Although his business was real estate, he knew about show business since his father was silent movie actor Earl Rodney. Luckily for both Marie and Jack, this marriage would not be dissolved by annulment or divorce for would last until death did them part. When Marie wed, she also become a stepmother to Jack's son Chris from a previous marriage.

Photos

Marie Windsor looking good and having fun.

Marie Windsor with children in *The Day Mars Invaded Earth*.

The Killing

15

ONE OF MARIE'S BEST PERFORMANCES ever was in the 1956 film entitled *The Killing*. The title does not refer to a murder but to an attempt by a bunch of crooks to make a major *financial* "killing." *The Killing* is about crook Johnny Clay (Sterling Hayden) who has just been released from prison. Johnny wants to make this "killing" so he will have the money to marry the woman he loves, Fay (Colleen Gray). Of course, penniless people can legally marry anywhere in the United States. But Johnny believed the two of them required a hefty nest egg to live comfortably and, presumably, to raise any children who happen to come along.

Johnny Clay plots the robbery of the proceeds at the Lansdowne racetrack. He gets together four confederates as the robbery team. Additionally, he hires two other men to commit acts in furtherance of the crime for a specified payment. One of those men is a fellow named Maurice Oboukhoff, a character with the odd distinction of being both a professional wrestler and a fine chess player. The man playing Maurice is Kola Kwariana who was actually both professional wrestler and a fine chess player! The other hireling is sharpshooter Nikki Arcane (Timothy Carey) who Johnny pays to kill one of the highest rated horses in the upcoming race, Red Lightning.

Clay believes he and his confederates will haul off $2 million that will be split five ways with four team members. Each person in this all-male team has his own reasons for participating. Bookkeeper Marvin Unger (Jay C. Flippen) is Johnny's close friend. Corrupt cop Randy Kennan (Ted de Corsia) needs to make payments to a loan shark. Track bartender

Mike O'Reilly (Joe Sawyer) has a wife, Ruthie O'Reilly (Dorothy Adams), who is dreadfully sick and bedridden so he wants money to pay for better medical care.

And then there is George Peatty, played by Elisha Cook, Jr. Not-so-gorgeous George is pivotal to the plot since he works at the track as a betting-window teller. George Peatty is self-conscious and timid. Superficially, at least, George does not seem the sort to participate in a big-time robbery. But he has a strong reason to go for the plan: he wants to provide a wealthy lifestyle for his lovely wife, Sherry, whom Marie plays with an inspired flair. Sherry is clearly disappointed in her husband and especially disappointed by the financial strain that is intrinsic to their lives and the cramped circumstances under which they.

Part of what makes Marie's performance in *The Killing* especially strong is that the personality of Sherry is more layered than that of the usual femme fatale. Esteemed critic Roger Ebert described Sherry as a "gold-digging floozy," a description not completely wrong but quite incomplete. Sherry is indisputably nasty in her condescending comments to George but there is an undercurrent in Marie's depiction of Sherry that makes her somewhat sympathetic, even a bit pitiful. Sherry feels trapped with George in a bleak existence lacking both passion and nice things. Sherry's gnawing sense of frustration at the limits under which she lives leads her to be caustic toward George. When he comes home, he asks what they are having for dinner. "Steak," she answers. "If you can't smell it cooking, it's because it's down at the supermarket."

George informs Sherry that their lives will soon improve greatly because George will be in possession of a large amount of cash. "Did you put the right address on the envelope when you sent it to the North Pole?" Sherry sarcastically inquires. She also tartly observes, "You don't have enough imagination to lie."

The way Marie plays Sherry, and the way the character is scripted, gives the perception that Sherry strikes out verbally at George not because she is "mean" in the sense of being cruel but because she feels being his wife dooms her to an existence that is "mean" in the sense of being confined to a "mean" level of resources. Indeed, Marie's playing of Sherry is a great deal more complex than is the playing of the typical femme fatale and this helps lend the character a special interest. Many years later Marie discussed how she approached her role as Sherry: "I never believed that Sherry meant to be so cruel, but she felt that life hadn't given her a fair shake and she was determined that it would." She added, "I tried to approach it from that point of view"—and she did, making Sherry an unusually memorable femme fatale.

Interestingly, it was Marie's dynamically nasty performance in *The Narrow Margin* that led to her casting in *The Killing*. Director Stanley Kubrick was searching for the right actress to play Sherry Peatty when he saw *The Narrow Margin*. "That's my Sherry," he said to co-producer James B. Harris—the pair had formed the Harris-Kubrick Films that would produce *The Killing*—indicating Marie Windsor.

The Encyclopedia of Stanley Kubrick by Gene D. Phillips and Rodney Hill asserts that *The Killing* "marks the true beginning of [Kubrick's] career." It is based on a novel entitled *Clean Break* by Lionel White. Kubrick and "hard-boiled" crime novelist Jim Thompson wrote the script.

In *The Killing*, Johnny and the other members of the robbery gang have planned the heist to occur during the running of the day's seventh race. In creating the movie, Kubrick followed the pattern of White's novel by quickly cutting between characters and their machinations. Phillips and Hill write that this technique "builds suspense with great intensity." There is an unseen and unnamed narrator giving voiceover to the events.

Roger Ebert believes that "the narrative itself is so labyrinthine we abandon any hope of trying to piece it together" but just enjoy "letting it happen" before our eyes. Ebert discerns, "Perhaps a motif can be found in the movie's storefront chess club." After all, Kubrick was a fine chess player and often frequented a storefront chess club as a youngster. Ebert writes that "chess involves holding in your mind several alternate possibilities" and believes "Johnny Clay has devised a strategy seemingly as flawless" as a fine chess game but notes that the plan he has made "depends on all the players making the required moves on schedule." And that leaves open the possibility that the slightest deviation from either move or timing could lead to disaster.

Phillips and Hill assert that scenes between the wimpy George and contemptuous Sherry constitute "some of the strongest dramatic scenes in the movie." Writing in *Contemporary Cinema*, Penelope Houston aptly called Elisha Cook Jr.'s usual persona "the prototype of all sad little men." All-too-aware of his own limitations—and reminded of them by Sherry's sharp tongue—George is obsessively afraid that Sherry might find a man she prefers to him. The audience learns early that his fears are realistic and that she is enjoying a romance with a criminal named Val (Vince Edwards). Kubrick may have cast Edwards as Sherry's boyfriend in part because in real life Edwards was almost a decade younger than Marie.

This makes it believable that she is desperately insecure about his love for her. She tells Val that she called him multiple times the previous evening and he failed to answer. Was he with another woman? He tells her he just likes to be out and about every now and then and admonishes her not to be "greedy." Sherry vows that she loves him so much it makes her a "glutton" for him.

There is a sense in which the Val-Sherry relationship is a reversal of George-Sherry. George will do anything to hold onto Sherry and try to give her the financial comfort she craves; Sherry is eagerly submissive to Val and hopes she can let him in on a secret that will securely bind the two together. She is also jealous, suspicious that there are other women in his life, precisely because she is so insecure about her hold on Val.

In both relationships, there is something all-too-believably sad about the way love enslaves one person to another. It is also true that the Val-Sherry romance underlines Sherry's basic weakness, making her softer, and sadder, than a typical femme fatale.

George's desire to hold onto his dear Sherry, and to lead her to believe they have a good future together, overcomes caution and he lets her know about the robbery.

A scene between Sherry and Johnny is notable for its witty repartee. Wanting to know more about the way the robbery will take place, Sherry eavesdrops on the group as they go over preparations. George assures his pals that he told her nothing about the planned crime but that she must have found the address in a piece of paper in his pocket and "thought I might be playing around with another dame." Johnny sends all the confederates away so he can deal with Sherry by himself. The conversation has a tinge of threat on Johnny's side and an undercurrent of flirtation from both characters. "That's a mighty pretty head you've got on your shoulders," Johnny points out. "Do you want to keep it there or start carrying it around in your hands?" "Maybe we could compromise and put it on your shoulder," Sherry suggests. When she affirms George's story that she was just checking up to see if he was two-timing her, Johnny scoffs. Sherry says he is unfamiliar with her. "I know you like a book," he retorts. "You're a no-good nosey little tramp." He asserts that Sherry would betray her own mother "for a piece of fudge" and that she has "a great big dollar sign where most women have a heart." He allows her to leave with her pretty head still on her shoulders because he believes she will keep quiet rather than disturb plans that will lead to her having riches.

The Killing can be seen as possessing more than one climax. Sherry's tip to Val leads to a shoot-out with several corpses strewn including Val's. George, who has shown himself quite adept with a gun, is left alive but mortally wounded. He manages to make it home where he finds Sherry cheerfully packing a suitcase. "Val, darling?" she says cheerfully. Then she turns around and her smile disappears. The audience easily reads her mind: Oh, no, it's you, George!

"Why, Sherry?" the betrayed George asks.

"I love you, Sherry," he says shortly before shooting and killing her.

In a lesser actress, Sherry's dying words, spoken as she clutches her wounded stomach and just before falling to the floor, would have struck a jarringly false note but Marie manages to deliver them with a pained power: "It's not fair. I never had anyone but you—not a real husband, not even a man, just a bad joke without a punchline."

After this, there is a second, more ultimate climax when Johnny and his girlfriend Fay believe they have "the killing" of their riches but the most unexpected of accidents shows them how even the most meticulously planned crime can go sickeningly wrong. Kubrick is far from a moralist but crime is shown not to pay and Johnny, in a moment of utter despair, accepts an awful fate. Circumstances have made a complete fool of him and he knows it.

The Killing was not a major moneymaker when it first came out. John Baxley writes in *Kubrick: A Biography* "After two years, *The Killing* would only have earned $30,000, and Harris would sell his and Kubrick's 50 per cent share to UA [United Artists] in return for the money to acquire *Lolita*."

However, the movie won praise from diverse quarters. *Time* magazine asserted of *The Killing* that "the camera watches the whole shoddy show with the keen eye of a terrier stalking a pack of rats" and compared Kubrick to the legendary Orson Welles. *Daily Variety* lauded the film as "tense and suspenseful," *The New York Times* asserted that "things move at a lively clip," and *The Daily News* called it "filled with suspense." *The New York World-Telegram and The Sun* singled out this book's subject for praise: "Marie Windsor is flamboyantly brash and sexy!" *Look* magazine gave her its Best Supporting Actress Award for her performance as Sherry. Marie very much appreciated that award, calling it, "My happiest moment as an actress."

Marie gave Stanley Kubrick high marks as a director. She recalled that, in her experience, he never yelled or threw tantrums but directed in a restrained and kindly manner. "When he had some idea for me to do or change something, he would wiggle his finger and we would go away from the action and he would tell me what he wanted," she remembered. "He didn't direct you in front of the crew." Marie has also commented on Kubrick's restrained manner, saying, "Though I'm sure Stanley Kubrick was full of energy, he didn't seem like it because he was so quiet and he moved very calculatingly—rather slow physically." Discussing him in a documentary, she said the then-young Kubrick that she worked with on *The Killing* "was a kid with tremendous confidence." Marie also praised Kubrick for paying close attention to details. For example, when George walks in on Marie reading a magazine, Kubrick told her, "I want you to move your eyes when you're reading." Sterling Hayden had little in common with the psychopath he played in *The Killing*, at least according to Marie. "He was a gentleman, soft-spoken, a very sweet man, a sort of almost tender fellow," she remarked. "I never saw another side to him." Marie became friends with Elisha Cook, Jr. when they made *The Killing*. She said both were glad to be working together as their "paths had crossed several times through the years."

This might be a good time to make the point that this "film noir" actress, and other film noir performers, did not call these movies by that term at the time they worked on them. Although the term "film noir," literally "dark film," was coined by a French critic in 1946, it took many years to catch on a standard phrase. "I didn't know I was doing film noir," Marie remembered. "I thought they were detective stories with low lighting! Even Kubrick, in 1955 during the filming of *The Killing*, never used the term film noir to my knowledge."

16

1957 SAW MARIE in *The Unholy Wife, The Parson and the Outlaw, The Girl in Black Stockings*, and *The Story of Mankind*.

The Unholy Wife is an obvious—and sadly ill-made—rip-off of *The Postman Always Rings Twice*. Diana Dors plays Phyllis, single mother of a child named Mike, who marries vineyard heir Rod Steiger in part to get a Dad for her kid and a roof over both their heads. Soon bored with paunchy Steiger, she carries on a backstreet affair with cowboy stud Tom Tryon. The film is poorly written and directed, slow-moving, and lacking in suspense. About the only good thing is the glamorous appearance of Diana Dors who is eye candy with her wavy platinum blond hair and tight-fitting brightly colored outfits. In a bit part, Marie is a friend to Phyllis and she also looks pretty and glamorous. Perhaps her best acting in this flick was when Dors deliberately drops her purse to get Steiger's attention and Marie looks appropriately bemused at the common flirting tactic.

Written by Oliver Drake and John Mantley, directed by Oliver Drake, *The Parson and the Outlaw* certainly starts from an interesting premise. The audience sees a funeral being held for that notorious thief and gunslinger, none other than Billy the Kid (Anthony Dexter). Reverend Jericho Jones (Buddy Rogers) expresses displeasure toward Marshal Pat Garrett (Bob Duncan) for the killing that led to the funeral. The gun belt of the famous outlaw is draped over his headstone and the mourners disperse.

Then Billy the Kid comes out from behind a tree! He is quite alive. The gun fight that Billy supposedly lost was actually the result of a theatrical fight staged by old pals Pat and Billy. The latter wanted to fake his own death and begin a new life as a peaceful and law-abiding homesteader. The pals say their goodbyes and a hopefully rehabilitated Billy, having put his bad side into the ground, heads to the town of Four Corners and a fresh start. In that town, he has bought a ranch as "Bill Antrum." On the trail on his way to Four Corners, Billy encounters a group of hostile American Indians threatening gun fighter Jack Slade (Sonny Tufts). Bill helps save Jack from the group. As the pair talk when the coast is clear, Bill learns that Jack is tracking Billy the Kid whom he plans to challenge to a gunfight. Bill informs Jack that he is too late: Billy the Kid is dead. Jack is disappointed but agrees to accompany his new friend to Four Corners.

As the pair of gunslingers (one supposedly reformed) rides into town, they find the town's founder, a corrupt man named Colonel Jefferson Morgan (Robert Lowery), shooting newspaper editor Matt McCloud (Kenne Duncan) because the editor had used his paper to advocate that Four Corners become part of Texas. Morgan strongly believes that, since he founded Four Corners, it should remain his own sort of fiefdom and has hired gunslingers like Ace Jardin (Bob Steele) to enforce his will. Jack Slade sees a use for his services and his offer of them is accepted by Morgan. Our newly reformed "Bill Antrum" buys ranch supplies at Four Corners.

In the wake of McCloud's death, his daughter Elly McCloud (Madalyn Trahey) vows to continue the fight to win annexation to Texas in an upcoming election. Billy discovers that Morgan minions are squatting on his ranch but Billy refuses to take sides in the annexation controversy.

Then who should arrive in town but Rev. Jericho Jones and his wife Sarah (Jean Parker)? The minister is stunned to discover that the man for whom he held funeral services is alive! Rev. Jericho wants to expose Bill Antrum as Billy the Kid; wife Sarah talks her husband into keeping quiet.

Billy finds Jack Slade, Ace Jardin, and others who work for McCloud enjoying a poker game on Antrum's property. He orders the poker players to do their thing somewhere else. Jack recalls how Billy rescued him from the Indians and suggests to his pals that they should indeed skedaddle. But Ace Jardin is not about to back down. He pulls a gun on Jack who is quicker on the draw and kills Ace. The dead man leaves behind his girlfriend Tonya, the character Marie plays. She asks Bill Antrum to take her on as a housekeeper and he is happy to hire someone to perform domestic chores.

Meanwhile, Elly McCloud diligently puts out the town's newspaper. Morgan's minions brutally beat Ben (Joe Sodja) because he is the paper's printer. The townspeople beg Rev. Jericho for help. The minister in turn asks Bill Antrum/Billy the Kid for help but he does not want in the fight.

Elly says she must find a courageous man to battle the Morgan gang and Rev. Jericho suggests Billy. Elly appeals to outlaw-turned-homesteader and he again says he wants to keep clear of the dispute. Tonya gets into a squabble with Elly. Billy dismisses Tonya for disrespecting the other woman. Then he drives the fired former employee into town in his wagon. In town, Jericho once again asks for the ex-gunslinger's assistance in fighting the Morgan gang. Billy recalls the terrible life he had as a fugitive and explains that he is desperate for a peaceful life. The minister requests that Bill attend a prayer meeting on the upcoming Sunday.

Sunday arrives and Morgan comes in with his gunslingers whom he orders to disrupt the service. At his orders, the bunch also shoots up the newspaper office. Cavalry arrive at the violence plagued town to restore order. Once again, Elly begs Billy for his assistance. He returns home to discover his cabin going up in flames. Tonya, the housekeeper he dismissed, is also there—severely injured because Morgan's men whipped her. Jack Slade rides up and warns Billy to leave town. Tonya asks Jack to take her back to town. A few more plot turns occur before the story concludes. The film ends with a written epilogue about Billy the Kid.

Made in the era in which women were "girls" until they were graying and wrinkled, *The Girl in Black Stockings* (1957) is a cheaply made but entertaining mystery written by Michael Landau and directed by Howard W. Koch. It starts with dancing people massed on the lawn of the Parry Lodge in Kanab, Utah. David Hewson (Lex Barker), a vacationing attorney from California, is dancing with pretty Beth Dixon (Anne Bancroft), a lodge employee, and making sweet talk with her. Ah, romance is in the air! Then Beth lets out a horrified scream. David, the others assembled, and the movie audience all see a brutally murdered female body. We soon learn that the murder victim, who has been hideously slashed with a knife, is Marsha Morgan, a "party girl" type. Investigators Sheriff Jess Holmes (John Dehner) and Judge Ben Walters (David Dwight) are soon on the job trying to ferret out the murderer. No sooner do they begin looking for the murderer of Marsha Morgan than bodies start piling up. Some twisted individual is clearly on a tear (pun unintended).

Early on we meet the sad owners of the Parry Lodge. Edmund Parry (Ron Randell) is an embittered quadriplegic. He despises flirtatious women and seems to think the victim got her just desserts. Marie plays his sister Julia Parry, who has sacrificed a normal life to care for her disabled brother. She appears utterly devoted to her brother, willing to spend her whole life feeding him and attending to his every need.

It will be revealed that Edmund became disabled shortly after a woman broke off her romance with him but the exact cause is ambiguous. It could have been the result of a stroke in which case he is ruled out as a suspect. Then again, it could be psychosomatic, in which case he might go through phases in which he—perhaps without even being consciously aware of it—regains the use (or partial use) of his limbs.

Sheriff Holmes questions David Dwight closely on his whereabouts. He was with Beth when the body was found but where was he earlier when Marsha was murdered?

Despite the Parry Lodge enduring such bad publicity, a new guest named Joseph Felton (Gene O'Donnell) checks in.

Other characters closely questioned by the Sheriff include aging and alcoholic actor Norman Grant (John Holland) who hopes to dry himself out at the Parry Lodge and make the classic screen comeback. His lovely actress wanna-be and girlfriend, Harriet Ames, is played by blonde bombshell Mamie Van Doren.

An alcoholic Native American named Joe (Larry Chance) is found with a blood-stained knife. It is learned that the knife was lifted from the Parry Lodge kitchen—and used in the murder. However, investigation shows that Joe had an ironclad alibi. Sheriff Holmes wonders if Joe might know more than he is telling or might have forgotten seeing something important during a drunken stupor.

Part of Beth's job is operating the lodge switchboard. While doing so, she overhears Joseph Felton talking to someone. Shortly after that, Felton is shot and falls into the Parry Lodge swimming pool where he drowns.

Holmes tells David that an alibi clears Joe and that the murdered Felton was a private detective. Holmes also reveals how a romance-linked trauma led to Edmund Parry's paralysis.

In a romantic interlude, Beth recounts the story of her life to David. She married when very young. That did not work out and she drifted through life until she found her work at the Parry Lodge. David assures her he is unconcerned about the past but only wants to love her in the present and future.

Sheriff Holmes appears at a lumber mill to question a worker, Frankie Pierce (Gerald Frank), who may have had a fling with Marsha. A panicky Pierce backs into a woodcutting machine and is torn to pieces. Guilt? Remorse? Did Sheriff Holmes find the murderer?

Edmund and sister Julia have a dinner party. Guests include Norman Grant and Harriet Ames. Harriet gets a little tipsy and flirts with the paralyzed Edmund who is clearly offended. Perhaps even more offended is devoted sister Julia who conscientiously wipes Harriet's offending lipstick from the side of Edmund's face.

Later that evening, cops are summoned to the Parry Lodge, finding Grant with a wound to his head—and Harriet viciously murdered in a manner very similar to how Marsha was murdered. A doctor tells Sheriff Holmes it is unlikely Grant could have inflicted the head wound on himself.

David drives to the Parry residence and finds Edmund alone. From Edmund, David learns something chilling about devoted sister Julia. According to Edmund, Julia was instrumental in the break-up that preceded his paralysis. However, he has forgiven her and will stand by her no matter what she has done.

Could this guilt-infused love for her brother have turned into a hate for flirtatious women? Could it have led Julia to serial murder?

Only at the very end do we find the true identity of the murderer.

Marie's portrayal of the self-sacrificing sister contains enough ambiguity to keep the audience guessing about what is really on Julia's mind.

Another film released in 1957, *The Story of Mankind,* may well have been the weirdest flick Marie ever participated in and lays claim to being one of the wackiest movies ever made. Irwin Allen directed it and co-wrote the script with Charles Bennett with both of them basing it on a book by Henrik Van Loon. The story begins by informing us that a Super-H bomb has been invented that could wipe out humanity. The Great Court of Outer Space holds a session to decide whether or not humanity should just be allowed to exterminate itself. The devil, called Mr. Scratch and played by Vincent Price, argues that humans should become extinct. The Spirit of Mankind, a character played by Ronald Colman, wants humans to continue. The audience is brought through a history course as each makes his case. Through this odd concept, this ambitious motion picture aims to give its viewers a comprehensive college course in history. Wagner observes that it has "a reputation as one of Hollywood's most notorious all-star bombs." Along with the aforementioned Price and Colman, this poorly regarded flick featured such respected performers as Peter Lorre, Cedric Hardwicke, Cesar Romero, Virginia Mayo, Marie Wilson, Hedy Lamarr, John Carradine, Agnes Moorhead, and Marx Brothers Harpo, Groucho, and Chico. It also included Dennis Harper as Napoleon and Marie as Josephine. In a scene between the couple, she gushes when found he has been "given the command." At one point, she playfully observes, "Modesty is not one of your virtues." She is splendid in her costume apparel but there is not much for her to do but admire her husband until he mentions becoming emperor and she remonstrates, "No, no! We fought a revolution for liberty and equality!" When she continues that a "king must be born," he replies that an "emperor can be elected."

A contemporary *New York Times* review of *The Story of Mankind* called it "a protracted and tedious lesson in history that is lacking in punch, sophistication and a consistent point of view." The reviewer noted the "battery of 'name' actors" and the "handsome sets to move through and tasteful costumes to wear" but concluded that the movie "has not succeeded in dramatizing what is essentially a disconnected pageant that ranges over every known period of history." A (probably) more recent review by Craig Butler called the film "so dull, almost relentlessly so, that it's hard to believe Allen was paying any attention to what was going on." Years after *The Story of Mankind* was released, co-scriptwriter Bennett called the movie "dreadful." Marie thought the idea behind it was good but acknowledged that the execution left much to be desired. "It's the kind of idea that demands top-notch quality with better writing and production values than our film got," she commented. "In some ways, it almost seemed like a glorified high school movie with a great cast." She has only two and a half minutes to appear in her role as Josephine but she acquitted herself quite ably. This author agrees with Laura Wagner that Marie and Dennis Hopper made of their short interchange "a powerful, restrained vignette, worthy of a better movie."

At studio mogul Jack Warner's request, Marie tested for the part of Vera Charles in *Auntie Mame*. However, she lost out to Coral Browne.

Marie's appearance in so many B-movies led to her being called the "Queen of the Bs." It was an appropriate designation since she rarely was offered parts in top-of-the-line motion pictures but was very busy in "B" movies. During the 1950s, television was coming into its own as a mode of entertainment and Marie divided her professional energies between the big screen and the small. Beginning in the 1960s and continuing until her retirement, Marie appeared more often on TV and movies. Television was attractive to Marie: "I wanted to work and TV had faster turnaround and quicker paychecks."

17 Television Triumphs

A GOOD EXAMPLE of her TV work is *The Red Skelton Hour*. In the late 1950s and early 1960s, Marie appeared in eight episodes alongside the legendary comic actor Red Skelton. *The Red Skelton Hour* showcased Marie's comedic talents in "The Picnic" (1956), "San Fernando's Showboat" (1957), "Freddie and the Brooklyn Dodgers" (1957), "Cauliflower's Hamburger Stand" (1958), "Freddie and the Millionaire" (1958), "Deadeye and the Magician" (1960), "The Great Brain Robbery" (1961), and "Appleby's Bearded Boarder" (1962).

"The Picnic" skit had Red depicting Bolivar Shagnasty, a loudmouth and braggart. Arthur O. Bryan plays Bolivar's boss and Marie plays the boss's daughter.

In "San Fernando's Showboat," Red Skelton played crooked politician San Fernando Red and Marie was his daughter, Jenny Lou. The skit commences with dancers aboard a showboat singing about a showboat. Then on comes mustachioed San Fernando smoking a slim cigar. He announces, "It is my pleasure to introduce to you the flower of the Mississippi River, my daughter Jenny Lou." Clad in 19th Century "Southern Belle" attire, Marie runs out from the side onto the stage.

Humorous exchanges follow with the daughter pitching questions and father saying punchlines.

"How can you tell the difference between a girl from the North and a girl from the South?" Marie's Jenny Lou sweetly drawls.

"You ask them for a kiss and the girl from the North will say 'you may' and the girls from the South will say 'you all may'" Red Skelton's San Fernando replies.

Jenny Lou: "What did Mr. Mason say to Mr. Dixon?"

San Fernando: "We gotta draw the line somewhere."

Jenny Lou hands out tickets to a stage show and San Fernando has a comical scene playing poker against Cameron Forsythe (Charles Ruggles). As one might expect, this is not a poker game played with scrupulous honesty as what comic value would you wring out of that?

Cut to Beauregard Forsythe (George N. Neise) wooing our sweet flower of the Mississippi. Beauregard: "I've been waiting most of my life for you." Jenny Lou: "I've been waiting for you, too."

The young couple and their elders, including Mrs. Forsythe (Isabel Randolph), are soon assembled together. Gazing at his adored Jenny Lou, Beauregard says, "I want to toast the most charming, the loveliest, the most gracious and intelligent creature in all the South."

"And after we drink to me, we'll drink to my daughter," San Fernando says as the audience laughs.

But there is no doubt that among those assembled on the stage, Marie Windsor is most apt to please the eyes.

Perhaps no Red Skelton character was more hilarious than hobo Freddie the Freeloader, who resided in the city dump and was often threatened with an arrest for vagrancy when snoozing on a park bench. Don Drysdale appears as himself in the episode entitled "Freddie and the Brooklyn Dodgers." Marie guests as herself on the show as do Marilyn Maxwell and Lyle Talbot.

"Cauliflower's Hamburger Stand" had Red playing Cauliflower Mc-Pugg, a boxer who was often punch drunk and, when in that state, given to hearing things. Marie was a character called Ruthie.

"Freddie and the Millionaire" showcases Charles Ruggles as Mr. Jennings, Anne Dore as Mrs. Jennings, and Marie as their niece.

Cactus Kate is the colorful name of Marie's character in the Old West-themed skit "Deadeye and the Magician." Deadeye is the town Sheriff, Vincent Price is the Maxwell the Magician, and Marie is the "saloon girl" named Cactus Kate. Maxwell the Magician uses his knowledge of sleight of hand to rob. Seated at a table in the saloon, an elaborately garbed Cactus Kate wails, "I wonder if he's robbed me!" She lifts her frilly skirt and finds to her horror that no cash is attached to the garter on her thigh! But Deadeye finds it hard to slap the handcuffs on Maxwell who has attached fake hands to his own.

In the two last *Red Skelton Hour* episodes in which she appeared, Marie was Clara Appleby, bossy wife who oppresses husband George Appleby. "The Great Brain Robbery" drew its title from the early silent movie of 1903 called *The Great Train Robbery* which related varied storytelling techniques to its viewers. "Appleby's Bearded Boarder" has John Carradine playing Abdul Kashmir complete with ubiquitous turban. Abdul Kashmir is a kind of nutritional guru who suggests George and Clara Appleby will benefit from a diet of one lima bean three times a day. Dressed in average mid-Century women's attire, Marie accepts this bizarre diet but George does not. Some jokes would be forbidden today as George calls the guest "rag head" and also ridicules the turban by asking, "Isn't your hair dry yet?" But the real humor derives from having George and Clara with single lima beans on their plates while Abdul has a nice juicy steak on his!

Marie played on four episodes of the far more serious TV show *Perry Mason*. In 1958, she played murder suspect/betrayed wife Linda Griffith on the episode entitled "The Case of the Daring Decoy." She was murder victim Flavia Pierce in 1960 in "The Case of the Madcap Modiste." 1962 saw her depicting Edith "Edie" Morrow in "The Case of the Tarnished Trademark." In the 1964 episode "The Case of the Wednesday Woman," Marie was Helen Reed.

"The Case of the Daring Decoy" has two men battling over control of an oil company. The rivals are Daniel Conway (H. M. Wynant) and Warner Griffith (John Mack Brown). At Conway's office, he finds an employee, Rose Calvert (Pamela Duncan) in there. He wants to know what her business is there and she explains she is only there to help straighten the office. Conway suspects she is snooping on behalf of his rival. She denies it but the audience sees her calling Warner to inform him she has possession of documents valuable to him. In another scene, Dan is searching for documents he wants when in walks Amelia Armitage (Jacqueline Scott). She informs him that she knows about Warner Griffith's plan to take the company from him and adds that she thinks the plan will harm stockholders. After Armitage exits, Dan answers a ringing phone. A woman gives him elaborate directions to get a list of the proxies Warner plans to use in his plot. One thing he must do is go to a room of the Hotel Redfern. In the hotel elevator, he encounters elevator operator Mavis Jordan (Natalie Norwick) who is so absorbed in the book she is reading that she fails to even look at him. Once he gets to the hotel room, he finds Rose—dead. Events soon lead to Dan Conway being charged with murder. However, since this is a *Perry Mason* episode, it goes without saying that there are other suspects. One of them is Warner Griffith's wife, Linda Griffith, Marie's character. At one point, she shows Perry a photograph her hubby took of his girlfriend. I will not be giving too much away when I point out that this episode has an interesting twist: the elevator operator identifies elevator users by their shoes!

In "The Case of the Madcap Modiste" Marie depicts Flavia Pierce, the "madcap" dress designer of the episode's title. And madcap Flavia most certainly is. The episode is hardly underway when Flavia is on a TV show (*within* the TV show *Perry Mason!*) with her husband Charles Pierce. She startles hubby with the revelation that she will not go along with a proposed business deal—which is vitally important to Charles who is thunderstruck at being contradicted by his wife in front of about 20 million TV viewers. Why would Flavia cause Charles consternation in this way? Subsequent scenes indicate she is jealous of his attraction to fashion model Hope Sutherland (Leslie Parrish). The designer who was behind the dashed deal, Henry De Garmo (David White, famous as Larry Tate on the sitcom *Bewitched*) tries to persuade Flavia's brother, George Halliday (Edward Mallory), to in turn persuade sis to revive the deal. Before any violence has been committed, Charles Pierce consults lawyer Perry Mason about the situation, having the attorney review business contracts and their prenuptial contract. Soon after this, Hope gives Charles a bottle of champagne. Flavia drinks that champagne and almost immediately falls to the floor. As Marie-as-Flavia dies, she tells assistant Leona Durant (Dorothy Neumann) that she's been poisoned by Charles. Of course, the murder case falls into Perry's lap.

Of Danish background, furniture builder Axel Norstaad (Karl Swenson) has spent three decades building up his business in "The Case of the Tarnished Trademark." The episode finds him planning retirement and planning to donate money from the sale of his business to the charitable building of a children's hospital. Axel's heart has been won by Marie's character, Edith "Edie" Morrow. She is a promoter working with her exhusband Latham Reed (Phillip Terry). Axel believes he has a buyer who will keep up the good tradition of his business in Martin Somers (Dennis Patrick). Things go awry when Axel discovers that Somers is as crooked as a pretzel and that the con artist is trading on Axel's good reputation to use shoddy goods to make a fast buck. Somers is murdered and Axel is arrested for the murder. However, with Perry Mason as his attorney, the audience guesses it is unlikely he will be convicted!

"The Case of the Wednesday Woman" has as its title character a devoted wife, Katherine Stewart (Phyllis Hill), who visits her imprisoned husband, Phillip Stewart (Phillip Pine), every Wednesday. He is serving time for involuntary manslaughter because he killed a man in a fistfight. Phillip has only a month prior to parole—but he has refused to meet the wife who loves him during that month. She is baffled by his rejection. When he is paroled, Katherine consults Perry Mason because she fears Phillip is disturbed enough to do something that will get him jailed again. Could Perry act as a go-between for a plan to get Phillip a job on the east coast so he will stay out of trouble? She needs this assistance due to Phillip's refusal to talk with her. Soon after this consultation, private detective Jack Mallory (Michael Pate) contacts Katherine to ask her about the valuable Jakarta Diamond that disappeared from the business her husband worked at close to the time of the killing. Phillip gets his old job back at the firm of Reed and Webber. Oddly enough, the "Reed" of the company's title is the surname of the fellow Phillip killed. This arrangement does not sit well with Reed's widow who is Marie's character, Helen Reed. However, we later learn that Helen was not in love with her husband and found him a scoundrel. Various plot turns occur and Mallory is found murdered. Perry ably defends Phillip Stewart from a murder charge and, in the process, uncovers some surprising information concerning the killing for which he had been incarcerated.

Maverick was a TV series that spiced the Western genre with a touch of comedy. James Garner starred as Bret Maverick, an adept poker player who liked to play his favorite game on riverboats and saloons. Marie guested on this series twice, the first time in 1957 and the second in 1962. The 1957 was "The Quick and the Dead." In that episode, Maverick got burned when he won a poker game and a fellow paid him with stolen money. The show has a marshal looking for Maverick because he has stolen money and Maverick looking for the fellow who unloaded the stolen cash on him. Maverick's investigating leads him to a saloon run by Marie's character Cora. It also leads him into a battle between the notorious Doc Holliday (Gerald Mohr) and another man. An IMDb reviewer observed, "Marie Windsor, who was the queen of the noir bad girls, is just as evil and scheming [here] as on the big screen. And Mohr makes a menacing Doc Holliday." Another stated, "Movie buffs will recognize cult figure Marie Windsor as the casino boss. In typical Windsor fashion, she manages to be both commanding and coy, at the same time.… Note too, the sly innuendo between Bret and Cora (Windsor) as they greet a new day."

Marie's 1962 stint on *Maverick* was on an episode entitled "Epitaph for a Gambler." By this time, there was a recasting with hero "Bart" Maverick played by Jack Kelly. In this episode, Maverick wins a poker game, his prize being part-ownership of a gambling casino owned by Diamond Malone (Robert J. Wilke). Maverick learns that Lucky Matt Elkins (Don Haggerty) has been extorting money and does not want the gravy train to screech to a stop because the casino has changed ownership. Marie plays Kit Williams. One IMDb reviewer disliked the episode, saying, "This is one of those later episodes where the writers appeared to forget what show they were writing for." The writer continued that it "degenerates into a melodramatic western." That person concluded, "As a standard western this is okay but it is not a really good example of *Maverick*." Another reviewer noted the lack of comedy in the episode, then commented on Marie's Kit Williams, remarking, "Sexy Marie Windsor spins the wheel and pays losing numbers because her boss Diamond Dan is being blackmailed by Elkins." The same reviewer observed that Marie was pivotal to the plot of the episode when Kit Williams turns violent. Reviewer "Hal" of a website called *The Horn Section*, writes, "Marie Windsor, so memorable as Doll Brown in *Hellfire*, does what she can with her limited screen time as the woman who stands by her man."

18

A Badman and Island Women

MARIE APPEARED IN TWO 1958 theatrical releases, *Day of the Badman* and *Island Women*.

Day of the Badman is a Western in which a town and its people are torn as to the punishment which murderer Rudy Hayes (Christopher Dark) should receive. The standard sentence for a murderer in the Old West (at least according to the movies this author has seen) is death by hanging and Judge Jim Scott (Fred MacMurray) is apt to impose that sentence. But relatives of the convicted murderer—Charlie Hayes (Robert Middleton), Howard Hayes (Skip Homeier), and Jake Hayes (Lee Van Cleef) ride into town and suggest another way of dealing with the malefactor: banishment. A violence-prone bunch, they make it clear that mercy to a murderer might be the only way the town can avoid trouble. Muddying the situation is that the judge believes he will soon wed the love of his life, pretty Myra Owens (Joan Weldon), and learns late in the story that her heart now belongs to Sheriff Barney Wiley (John Ericson). Muddying the waters even further is Marie's character, Cora Johnson. She is in love with Rudy but he rejects her when he becomes convinced she ratted on him about the murder he committed. Although she loves Rudy, Cora used to have a romance going on with Jim Scott and tries to use the embers of their burned out love affair to promote leniency for Rudy. Later, she overhears a telltale conversation between Myra and the Sheriff and *does* rat about it to Judge Jim Scott. During the film, Marie is alternately sour, grim, flirtatious, hopeful, vindictive, and grief-stricken. A review in a website called *The Movie Scene* stated that the film had "elements [that] could have been built upon" to create "one of those rare westerns with character depth and emotional impact" but there was not enough development. Thus, it is "an ordinary and frankly forgettable walk through the basic western storyline" that includes "danger" and "the truth coming out" in a way that "borders on the inevitable."

Island Women is a very different sort of film. Marie starred along with Vince Edwards and Marilee Earle in this film. Earle plays young Jan who is traveling with Aunt Elizabeth, the character Marie plays. They take a trip to the Bahamas. They meet Mike (Vince Edwards), a handsome and lusty charter boat proprietor to whom both women are attracted. The eternal triangle is spiced with the inevitable envy of an older female for a younger one. It is shot on location in the Bahamas. A come-on tag line for the flick read: "The whole ripped-bare story of the beach babes of the Caribbean!"

Under the Knife

19

In discussing the film industry and the late 1940s through the 1950s, the topic of the notorious Hollywood Blacklist often comes up. Marie was never blacklisted nor did she ever feel in any danger of being blacklisted. She was never drawn to communism or anything close to it. Her political sympathies varied, with some positions being liberal but, overall, she considered herself a political conservative.

Marie went under the knife for cosmetic reasons in 1959. She had a rhinoplasty, popularly called a "nose job," because she believed her nose was "too prominent." However, she later questioned that decision, wondering if she might have gotten more sympathetic roles with her original nose. Unfortunately, no one can ever undo cosmetic surgery but only have another cosmetic surgery. There is no evidence Marie tried to change her nose again which is probably for the best as repeated cosmetic surgeries can often cause special problems and a false appearance. Nevertheless, Marie believed that—as lovely as she indisputably was—her appearance prevented her from reaching A-list stardom. "A lot of things hampered my career," she asserted. "I never had a classic face. One of my acting directors at Paramount said, 'Her eyes are too big and she has a bad mouth.'" Of course, the casting director was wrong. Marie's eyes were one of her most beautiful features and large eyes are generally considered beautiful. Still, there was a "predatory" aspect to those eyes that fit well with unsympathetic characters. Her mouth was far from "bad" but looked sensual.

By the time of the 1960s, Marie was working primarily on television although she did not completely abandon the big screen. In 1962, she won a place on the board of directors of the Screen Actors Guild. She would hold that position for decades.

One aspect of Marie's career that should be addressed is the effect aging had on it. All-too-many actresses not only age out of leading roles but age right out of entertainment careers when they hit their forties. Indeed, it is not at all uncommon for careers to be brief because an actress makes a splash as an ingenue or sexpot and almost immediately ages out of that type of role.

Marie's roles changed when she entered middle age but she continued to be cast frequently and in varied roles. There may have been two reasons why her career continued strongly even as it changed while those of all-too-many others fizzled out as the skin began to crease and the hair to silver.

Firstly, Marie may have benefited from her "B-list" status. Unlike a superstar, she never became so completely associated with a particular character or persona that the audience could not accept her in other types of roles.

Secondly, although her main fame was as femme fatales, her acting chops were such that she was believable in just about any role. Marie was credible as characters who wicked or virtuous, bitter or satisfied, callous or concerned.

Marie made some wryly humorous comments on the loosening of restrictions in the entertainment world that started in the 1960s.

It became almost fashionable for actresses to pose for magazines or do film scenes in the buff—but Marie did not participate in this trend. "I hate to admit this, because it really isn't a very classy statement but I never turned a picture down unless they asked me to *strip!*" she recalled. "So I'd take anything [clothed], unless it was too tiny. *Now* I don't care how tiny, I just would like to work."

And work she did, mainly on shows viewed in America's living rooms.

Marie acted on a 1960 episode of the wildly popular TV show *77 Sunset Strip.* In the series, Efrem Zimbalist Jr. plays an ex-secret service agent for the government who is now a private detective, Stuart "Stu" Bailey. Roger Smith played private detective Jeff Spencer. They had a private detective firm called Bailey and Spencer and were played as hip, promiscuous men adopting a "Rat Pack" style. Perhaps the "hippest" part of the show was valet parking attendant Gerald Lloyd Kookson, usually called "Kookie." He was played by Edd Byrnes and the depiction launched Byrnes into "teen idol" stardom. Kookie's good looks and vanity were underlined by the ubiquitous comb he carried to ensure not a hair was ever out of place. That comb became such a part of pop culture that it was the basis of a novelty hit record entitled *Kookie, Kookie, Lend Me Your Comb*. During the show's run, he graduated from parking cars to member of the detective agency.

"Collector's Item" was the title of the early 1960 episode on which Marie appeared, taking an aristocratic turn as Countess Maruska. She hires Jeff to take an especially precious sculpture to New York on her behalf. She believes the creator of it may be the renowned Auguste Rodin. Countess Maruska believes that he threw the sculpture away but, even if Rodin himself was dissatisfied by it, the item would be worth millions just because he had created it. Jeff is to take it to an art expert she respects to have it authenticated.

Jeff has the wrapped piece in his possession when he learns there are other people after it. Countess Maruska believes the others also know it could be a Rodin. However, when Jeff unwraps the piece, he suspects there could be another secret behind its alleged great value and must learn why he is really taking it to New York. An IMDb reviewer believes Marie lent a great deal to the episode, writing, "The case turns out to be a sort of espionage one, with Windsor as the femme fatale. Some good sequences, always very atmospheric, for this show. Especially the one between Windsor and Roger Smith, in the apartment, with the music score of the famous Warner Bros. movie, *Now, Voyager*. Even if the story itself is not so exciting, believe me, this short scene is worth the rest of the episode."

Marie guest starred in a Western TV series called *The Rebel* that first aired in 1960. This series centered around a Confederate veteran and aspiring author named Johnny Yuma who was played by Nick Adams. He travels through the American West, writing about his adventures in a journal.

"Glory" is the title of *The Rebel* episode in which Marie appeared. Glory is the name of another character, a saloon worker played by Jennifer Lea. Yuma finds her outside town, wandering and distraught. She tells him that the townspeople suspected her of murder. There were some who wanted to lynch her and, to prevent that, others just forced her out of town. Marie plays Emma Longdon, one of those who helped banish the young lady. Emma's brother Don Longdon (William Bryant) had been in love with Glory and wanted to marry her prior to the incident that led him to also believe Glory committed murder. Yuma returns to town where he encounters Emma and Don as well as other townspeople who are appalled that anyone would help Glory. Emma suggests Yuma has been "dazzled by that creature" as her brother once was. But Yuma forces Emma to accompany him and the two of them ride out to meet Glory. After Emma dismounts, Yuma gives Glory the horse and tells Emma to walk back into town, noting that it will be a far more reasonable walk than the walk she and others intended Glory to make. "I'll kill you for this!" Emma screams.

Back in town, she derides Yuma as "smart and mean," suggesting only Glory's feminine wiles would lead "a stranger to defy a whole town to help a cheap dancehall girl." Emma and Don saddle up and catch up with Glory and Yuma. "I want to be the one to kill her!" Emma shouts at one point.

The episode is basically a fairly standard Old West story. It is given a special flavor by the passion Marie invests in her performance as a woman fearful that the brother she loves could jeopardize his future with a woman unworthy of him.

Marie did two guest appearances, both in 1960, on the private detective series set in New Orleans called *Bourbon Street Beat*. Rex Randolph (Richard Long) and Cal Calhoun (Andrew Duggin) ran Randolph and Calhoun—Special Services along with their secretary Melody Lee Mercer (Arlene Howell). The series never attained the popularity of *77 Sunset Strip* and some other detective shows. The first episode in which Marie appeared, as a character called Veda Troup, was "The 10% Blues" about a so-called "talent agency" that tries to extort 10% from New Orleans performers. Perhaps the most interesting aspect of this episode is that baseball legend Sandy Koufax played a bit part as—of all things—a door-person. Marie's second *Bourbon Street Blues* stint was in the episode "Teresa." The episode revolves around Jan Dennison (Andra Martin) who wants the detectives to find her lost brother Brad Dennison (Richard Rust). That brother had been involved with Mara Lane, the character Marie depicts. Mara is the owner of a casino and, as might be expected of a casino owner, appears to have "connections." There is a special concern on Jan's part because she knows their rich father will disown Brad if the relationship with Mara is revealed to him. This leads to finding Brad on Mara's privately owned island (casino owners can bring in the big bucks) where she has been acting as hostess to a couple of big-time criminals who did a quarter of a million dollar bank robbery. Hey, where is a character called "Teresa"? There must be a "Teresa" since that is the episode's title, right? It turns out to be a some*thing* as Rex and Jan want to find Brad as Hurricane Teresa is hurtling through Louisiana and moving toward Mara's island.

An anthology program, *New Comedy Showcase*, aired in 1960. It was a "showcase" for unaired pilots. Marie was on "Johnny Come Lately," which was about the travails of TV newscaster Johnny Martin (Jack Carson). *The Times-Mail* of Bedford, Indiana reported on August 6, 1960, "In 'Johnny Come Lately,'" Carson plays Johnny Martin, popular newscaster, who will do just about anything to steal a 'beat' on the local newspapers. To get a behind-the-scenes exposé of a series of waterfront incidents, Johnny dons a sailor's uniform, which succeeds in getting him not only behind the scenes but also into a series of hilarious complications. Johnny's problems are multiplied by Miss Talbot, the television station censor, played by Miss Windsor, who insists on 'blue penciling' his material."

One of Marie's most sweetly memorable roles aired in the year 1960 on the beloved TV classic *Lassie*. "Little Cabbage" is the title of the November 1960 episode on which Marie guest starred—*as* a movie star! Of course, there is a kind of tradition of movie stars playing movie stars on both big screen and small.

The first scene of "Little Cabbage" opens with a car driving down a long and winding road. The driver suddenly loses control but little Timmy (Jon Provost) gets out of the way in time with the help of his trusty four-footed friend Lassie.

"Little one!" Marie cries in a high-pitched, breathy voice as she runs to Timmy. "Are you all right? Speak to me!" The child explains that he is fine thanks to the quick action of his dog, Lassie. Then the lovely woman who is elegantly attired with a broad-brimmed hat on her head and a fur piece draped across her shoulders cries out, "Oh, my baby!" She runs back to her car to pick up her poodle whom she gushes over. Lassie and Timmy follow and Timmy suggests she find help at his parents' house.

"And a little boy shall lead them!" Marie dramatically declares. When the foursome reach the house, she reveals that her name is Mimi Marlowe.

"The movie star?" Timmy's mom asks.

She is indeed Mimi Marlowe the movie star. However, Marie does not play her as any version of Marie Windsor the movie star. Instead, Marie does a semi-comic but endearing send-up of Zsa Zsa and Eva Gabor in her performance as Mimi Marlowe. As with "The Ring" in *Public Defender*, she brings a motherly warmth to the role in both her relationship with her poodle, whose name translated into English is "My Little Cabbage," and her interactions with Timmy.

A syndicated TV anthology drama was called *The Best of the Post* because its episodes were adapted from stories published in the *Saturday*

Evening Post. She was in "No Visitors," a 1961 episode in which a hospitalized writer learns the value of life from those around him including, presumably (I was unable to see the episode and could find little information about it) Marie's character, Nurse Simmons.

Marie appeared in an episode of *The Life and Legend of Wyatt Earp* that aired in 1961. *The Life and Legend of Wyatt Earp* was a very popular TV Western inspired by the life story of the actual Old West whose name is in the title. It ventured into unusual territory when it aired "Wyatt Earp's Baby." When the episode commences, Earp is on his way to Tucson for a meeting with the Governor when he finds a surprise: a wagon that was attacked and burned by Apaches. Earp finds a crying baby—an orphan because the infant's mother and father were killed. Since Earp is in Pima County, he takes the parentless baby to that county's Sheriff Slim Lydell (Frank Ferguson). The official refuses to assume custody of the baby because he believes it is Earp's own. Then Earp takes the baby to the character Marie plays, saloon manager Lily Henry. It is likely Marie brought her considerable mothering instinct to this role. Lily is happy to care for the baby while Earp meets the Governor and care for the child overnight as Earp searches for a couple to adopt the orphan.

Lily is aided in caring for the child by a male friend, Muley Boles (Sean McClory) who is the owner of a blacksmithing business as well as a freight business. Frustrated in his attempts to find prospective adoptive parents, Earp learns from Muley that Lily had a son and husband, both of whom died. Earp learns from Lily that Muley had his wife and son die. Lily and Muley continue to share the caring of the infant. Earp convinces them that they should marry and adopt the child with whom they have already bonded.

Whispering Smith was a Western TV series starring Audie Murphy as 19th century Denver, Colorado police detective Tom "Whispering" Smith. It ran into a certain controversy when the U.S. Juvenile Delinquency subcommittee called it overly violent. *The New York Times* ran a front page article on June 9, 1961 about a subcommittee hearing on the show. After the subcommittee watched an episode, Colorado's Senator John A. Carroll derided the show as "a libel on Denver." Partly because of the controversy, and partly because Audie Murphy became bored with playing on the show, it was canceled after twenty episodes.

Marie appeared on the 15th episode. In that episode, a serial murderer appears to be operating (several decades before "serial murderer" became a common phrase) as three Denver men are found murdered on consecutive days. Whispering Smith and others believe the same male-factor was responsible for the murders as all three victims had been shot between the eyes and, even more curiously, all three had had the third button on their vests removed! Our hero Smith finds a link to the owner of a popular casino, Marie's character Maple Gray. One can only wonder what Marie thought of owning a modern casino in *77 Sunset Strip* and a 19th century one in *Whispering Smith*!

Bronco was a Western TV series that also showed an ex-Confederate soldier wandering through the Old West. Bronco Layne was the protagonist played by Ty Hardin. In "The Equalizer," Butch Cassidy and Billy Doolin, together with their respective gangs, visit the town of Painted Rock to attend the wedding between Doolin's brother and Cassidy's niece. However, there are bad feelings between the two ruffians who have been feuding. U. S. Marshal John Heyes (James Seay) asks Bronco to help keep the peace. Marie plays a character called Belle Logan.

Marie spent much of her cinematic life in the fabled Old West and the *Lawman* TV series was yet another case of that. *Lawman* took place in Laramie, Wyoming starting in 1879 and continuing through the 1880s. John Russell was Marshal Dan Troop and Peter Brown played Deputy Marshal Johnny McKay. "The Wanted Man" was the episode in which Marie played Ann Jesse, wife of "wanted man" Frank Jesse (Dick Foran). In the episode, Marie is not required to show off her horseback riding or gun twirling skills. It starts off with Ann Jesse very far advanced in pregnancy—and very sick. She is in the back of a wagon as her son, Ben Jesse (Jane Stine), drives her into town. Marshal Troop and Deputy McKay find her; Ben returns with a doctor. Ben cannot have her moved to a better place since he has but a single dollar to pay the physician. A bounty hunter, Joe Street (Alan Baxter), rides into town, hoping to grab Frank Jesse and get the $5,000 reward on him. Marshal Troop tells Street he does not want the wanted man gunned down. Ann begs the Marshal not to arrest her husband if he voluntarily shows himself. At the doctor's urging, the "lawman" agrees. Frank Jesse arrives to see his baby born—and Ann die giving birth. Frank Jesse tells adult son Ben (Jan Stine) to turn him in to Marshal Troop so Ben might collect the $5,000 reward and use it to raise the motherless child. Troop finds himself in conflict with bounty hunter Joe Street (Alan Baxter) who wants to gun the "wanted man" down to get his hands on that reward.

Marie appeared in three *Rawhide* episodes, one airing in 1959, another in 1961, and the last in 1964. The 1961 episode bore the intriguing title "The Incident of the Painted Lady." The Western series starred Eric

Fleming as trail boss Gil Favor and Clint Eastwood as assistant Rowdy Yates. "The Incident of the Painted Lady" revolved around trouble because aggrieved townspeople wanted Favor to give them either 1,000 cattle or $15,000 because another Texas trail boss, Thad Clemens (David Brian) took 1,000 of their cattle on consignment and failed to return with it or give them money for it. Since Favor is also a Texas trail boss, they attempt to hold him responsible. Thus our hero seeks out Thad Clemens and the reasons Thad, who had previously enjoyed an impeccable reputation, had swindled people. There is a suggestion that he needed money for Miss Katie, the character Marie played. Well described as "all woman," Miss Katie owns and operates a saloon and gambling café combo called "The Painted Lady." It turns out that Thad Clemens tried to cover for his ne'er do well son, army Leiutenant Cory Clemens (Ed Nelson) who has a strong gambling itch and an even stronger attachment to the "painted lady" who owns "The Painted Lady." In this Western episode, Marie displays neither pistol nor horse skills. She remains in a dress, sometimes with a beauty mark ostentatiously on a cheek. At first a bit brusque, even off putting, Miss Katie wins audience sympathy when she talks about growing up as "a girl orphan in a country of men." In just a few scenes, we see her acting skills on full displays as the script calls for Miss Katie to alternate between sassy, saucy, defensive, fearful, loving, and self-sacrificing.

Paradise Alley

20

PARADISE ALLEY WAS THE NAME of a very special motion picture that was made in 1958 although it was not shown in movie theaters until 1962. It is the only movie released that year in which Marie appeared. It was also the last movie made by an unusual writer and director named Hugo Haas.

Hugo Haas was only one of a multitude of talented individuals who came to America to escape the rule of the Nazis. When Nazi Germany occupied Czechoslovakia in 1939, the National Theater fired him because of his Jewish background. Haas became an in-demand supporting actor in the 1940s. In the 1950s, he branched out into making a series of cheaply made B movies as a director and screenwriter. He often also acted in the films, often as an older and gullible man who falls for a conniving and faithless younger woman, usually a buxom blonde. In fact, this theme recurred so often in the films he wrote and directed that it is impossible not to wonder to what extent it reflected a personal fear, and/or sexually arousing fantasy, of his. Given the complications of emotions, it is quite possible that Haas was both frightened by the idea of a young lady taking advantage of him *and* turned on by it. The tall and slender Beverly Michaels starred in the Hugo Haas flick *Pick-Up* in which she plays a very down-on-her-luck impoverished woman who weds the Haas character for his relatively small "fortune" but soon finds herself entranced by a handsome stud nearer her own age. *Pick-Up* was surprisingly successful with the public. It was also cinematically important because it may have helped launch the 1950s cycle of "bad girl" movies. Haas team followed this film with *The Girl on the Bridge* that also starred Beverly Michaels. In this film, Michaels played a far softer and more sympathetic character than she had in *Pick-Up*. However, *The Girl on the Bridge* was not a success which might be a reason Haas ended the professional relationship with Michaels and turned to Cleo Moore as his leading lady. Moore had a more conventional blonde bombshell appearance than Michaels. The two made a string of movies. Moore was usually a gold-digging and faithless harpy á la *Pick-Up* but Haas sometimes cast her in more sympathetic roles such as the part she played in *Bait* of a widowed mother falsely believed to be a promiscuous "bad girl." Haas sometimes took a break from blonde bombshells like Michaels and Moore to cast brunette siren Carol Morris as his femme fatale.

Paradise Alley can be viewed as a kind of window into its creator's feelings. An IMDb plot summary of the film aptly begins, "As studio financing dwindled away for Hugo Haas, his last film as a writer-director-producer has certain autobiographical elements, a cast featuring several film veterans from the silent era, and a storyline containing a metaphoric commentary on Hollywood." Film veterans in this movie include, but are hardly limited to, performers who worked in silent films. Chester Conkline, Corinne Griffiths, Billy Gilbert, and Carol Morris as well as Marie play in *Paradise Alley*.

The story is set in a rundown tenement slum in which residents often bicker and young males congregate in the street to play various games. Although Carol Morris was in her 20s, she played a teenaged girl. Marie plays Linda Belita, an impoverished woman longing for glamour who interests the young men with her (by late 1950s standards) sexy shorts but gets bitterly lectured by another female slum dweller for her figure flaunting. Haas puts a cute joke in when he shows Mr. Nicholson (Tom Fadden) doing a crossword puzzle and wondering out loud about a negative term for a woman that ends with "ch." Mrs. Nicholson is played by Margaret Hamilton who made her greatest splash as The Wicked Witch of the West in *The Wizard of Oz*. "It wouldn't be 'witch,'" Mr. Nicholson muses. Then he decides it is "wench."

Mr. Angus is dismayed by the petty quarreling of his neighbors. He hits upon a way to draw them together and ensure cooperation. Mr. Angus announces to his neighbors that he is making a motion picture tentatively entitled *The Chosen and the Condemned* that will be set in the neighborhood with its residents as the cast. He "films" them with a camera that lacks film.

The plan works beautifully. The formerly bickering neighbors are so flattered at the idea of being in a movie that they put aside their differences and pull together. Ah… but what will happen when the people learn the whole thing is phony? It is easy to imagine them as crushed and angered when they learn they were deceived. Indeed, there is a hint of Norma Desmond from *Sunset Boulevard* believing she is about to make a comeback and Max ensuring she never learns the truth that movie studios simply have no interest in her.

Deux ex machina! A studio head gets wind of this project and gives Mr. Angus the funds to make an actual motion picture.

Hugo Haas died five years after completing *Paradise Alley*, at the age of 67. *Paradise Alley* was an appropriate swan song, being at once melancholy and sweet, realistic yet finally optimistic. It is a comment on the human condition itself and how, flawed as we are, we are also good.

Considering how many screen veterans played in *Paradise Alley*, it is significant that an advertisement for the movie billed over it, *Rome Adventure*, in *The Berkshire Eagle* of Pittsfield, Massachusetts, added, "Plus Marie Windsor in *Paradise Alley*."

Baby Break, Martian Mayhem

21

ALTHOUGH DEDICATED TO HER career throughout most of her life, Marie also possessed a powerful sense of domesticity. Her 1954 marriage had made her a wife and step-mother. Since shortly after marrying, she longed to bear her own child. That yearning was fulfilled on January 11, 1963 with the birth of Richard "Rick" Hupp. Although films in which she played were released in 1962 and 1963, she took a hiatus from both onscreen and stage work to prepare for having a baby.

The "baby break" lasted for a little over a year as it included most of her pregnancy plus the first six months of her baby's life. Away from Hollywood glamour, Marie cheerfully devoted herself to feedings and diaper changes, as well as bathing and dressing, cuddling and cooing the newcomer.

A motion picture released while Marie was home caring for baby Richard was the 1963 *Critic's Choice*. The film was a comedy starring two of Hollywood's greatest comedy performers, Bob Hope and Lucille Ball. It is good that it was a color film as color is best for showing off the red hair of its female star. Bob Hope plays theater reviewer Parker Ballantine, who is invariably delighted when panning a play but morose when honesty leads him to give a positive review. He is wed to housewife Angie Ballantine and they are raising Parker's son by a previous marriage. Over Parker's objections, Angie decides to try her hand at writing a play. She bases the play, a comedy, on the adventures she and her sisters had while growing up. Quite appropriately, she titles her play *Sisters Three*. The film is about three-quarters over when Marie makes her appearance. She plays Sally Orr, one of Angie's sisters. Marie handles her role with sophisticated aplomb as she says lines like "But it's different in Paris, darling!" and expresses pride in seeing "our story on Broadway." A hint of the sly comes through when Angie suggests she may leave Parker and Sally says *she* may take a crack at him since she is "between husbands."

The Day Mars Invaded Earth was also released in 1963. Directed by Maury Dexter, scripted by Harry Spaulding, this black and white science fiction flick borrows liberally from *Invasion of the Body Snatchers* (1956) and *The War of the Worlds* (1953) with a dash of *Village of the Damned* thrown in for good measure. It also prefigures Ira Levin's novel *The Stepford Wives* and all the *Stepford* cinematic treatments.

The film begins with a robotic surveyor apparently on the landscape of Mars. It starts to move around the Martian surface but then—presto!— it appears to be inexplicably destroyed by some sort of burst of energy.

Cut to NASA and mission control where the scientist leading the mission to Mars, Dr. Dave Fielding (Kent Taylor) experiences a sense of confusion and faintness as sudden as the destruction of the exploratory vessel. But he immediately perks up and leaves his office to greet the reporters who want to know about NASA's mission to the red planet.

Dave flies to California to spend time with his family. They are temporarily residing on an enormous estate with a suitably enormous mansion [in reality, the building that appears in the film is the historic Greystone Mansion] that is owned by his in-laws. His children, teenaged Judi (Betty Beall), and 10-year-old Rocky (Gregg Shank) are overjoyed to see Dad. Wife Claire, played by Marie, also greets him. However, we soon learn that the marriage is in trouble because Dave's job is so very demanding that Claire is left a kind of "space widow." She obviously loves her husband but is just as obviously disappointed by his neglect of her. A housewife who feels like a kind of single mother, she understandably needs more than to be a domestic aide to her husband and their kids.

An oddity of the flick is found in the budding romance between pretty teenager Judi and her boyfriend Frank Hazard (Lowell Brown). It is hardly surprising that the daughter of a scientist would be attracted to a youth who plans a career as a bacteriologist. But there is something a bit jarring about a "date" to a seminar on the effects of enzymes on a certain type of bacteria!

At any rate, things start getting spooky when the main characters begin encountering body doubles of themselves and other family members.

The explanation is that the NASA robotic machine did in fact encounter "Martians" of a very unexpected variety. An intelligent life form evolved on that planet but is not made of flesh and blood. Rather, the

Martians are a life form of pure energy. They experienced the NASA probe as a kind of invasion of their planet and they in turn invaded earth, seeking to take over the bodies of pivotal scientists—plus the scientists' family members since they might recognize the fakes—to stop further encroachment on their planet.

The Day Mars Invaded Earth appeared on double bills with other B movies. It was neither a whopping success nor a dismal failure with critics or audience. A brief contemporary review in the Pennsylvania newspaper *The Standard-Speaker* praised it as possibly "the most unusual story of the year." The premise, although not completely original, is interesting and the execution at least serviceable. It is well-acted by Kent Taylor and especially well-acted by Marie who is utterly natural as the loving but neglected housewife. As an IMDb reviewer noted, Marie's "performance is the standout" because "watching her on screen, it's possible to forget that you are watching actors getting paid for making believe they're someone they're not." Indeed, the point of good acting is believability and here, as so many times elsewhere, Marie perfectly fit that bill. A movie aficionado with whom the author of this book is well-acquainted was very impressed with Marie's performance in *The Day Mars Invaded Earth*. He is also a fan of *The Killing* and her work as disappointed femme fatale in that classic noir. "If I hadn't known in advance that it was the same actress playing Claire who played Sherry in *The Killing*, I never would have guessed it was the same actress," he told this writer. "She just looked and acted so different in the films that I couldn't tell it was the same person." That, of course, is the essence of *acting*.

Although she spent most of her time in 1963 caring for the little newcomer in diapers, she spent some of it on a political campaign. Along with several other Republican actresses, she made appearances for Republican presidential hopeful Senator Barry M. Goldwater. She must have been disappointed when he lost in a landslide to Democrat Lyndon B. Johnson.

Saloons, Brothels, and Other Places

In 1964's *Mail Order Bride* and 1969's *The Good Guys and the Bad Guys*, Marie played two different saloon keeper characters. Burt Kennedy directed both flicks and it is likely he liked her as the saloon owner so well in the former that he wanted her to essentially reprise it in the latter.

Mail Order Bride was a Western with an overlay of "Beauty and the Beast" as it is about a man being civilized, changed from a bad man to a good man, through marriage to a good woman. The elderly Will Lane (Buddy Ebsen), retired from law enforcement, was given the deed to a dying buddy's Montana ranch and told to give it to the man's son, Lee Carey (Keir Dullea) only if—hopefully *when*—the younger man abandoned his foolish ways. The dead man stated that Lee must marry before getting the ranch, apparently believing that marriage would help the youth settle down. Will Lane has the idea to find a bride through catalogue advertisements. He follows up the ads, finding woman after woman unsuitable. One is found unsuitable because she is unattractive as well as a devoutly religious Salvation Army soldier. Another is found unsuitable because, although lovely, she is devoutly religious and will only wed a man as Christian as she. A third is excluded due to her apparent "easy virtue." [The term is not used in the film; I used it because it seems appropriate to the time period in which it is set.] Finally, he happens upon Hanna's Saloon. Marie plays Hanna. She is ingratiating, beautifully attired, and confident but clearly out of the right age range for young Lee. But she has just the woman for a young man and sends employee Annie Boley (Lois Nettelton) off to teach the wild man to mend his ways. Although Marie is not onscreen for long, she makes enough of an impression on both Will and the audience that we are not surprised when we eventually find the older man returning to the saloon, presumably with marriage in mind.

Also a Western, *The Good Guys and the Bad Guys* found Marie managing yet another saloon. First hitting the theaters in 1969, it was directed by Burt Kennedy. The screenplay was co-written by Ronald M. Cohen and Dennis Shryack. The plot revolves around hero Marshal Flagg (Robert Mitchum), a law officer who is planning to retire when he discovers that McKay (George Kennedy), an outlaw with whom Flagg previously locked horns, is back in town and planning a major heist. Flagg to the rescue is impeded when he is captured by the McKay gang. When Flagg is held prisoner, he learns that the gang no longer considers the aging McKay their leader but have passed that baton to the younger Waco (David Carradine). In a display of his newfound and relished authority, Waco orders McKay to shoot Flagg. McKay is unable to bring himself to shoot the aging lawman. This leads to a confluence of brouhahas in the film's Old West. Marie plays Polly who, as noted, runs the saloon. Roger Ebert called *The Good Guys and the Bad Guys* "a fairly good Western but not good enough." He continued that it "tends to get bogged down in those slice-of-Western-life scenes that the new generation of directors seems to remember from old John Ford movies" and that "the movie never seems quite sure whether it's serious or not." Still, Ebert praises it for having "quite a climax." He writes that Marie, like some other supporting performers, plays "a good character role." *New York Times* reviewer Howard Thompson had a less generous view of the flick, writing, "There is nothing even mildly compelling about this anemic, fumbling and altogether aimless little exercise." He notes that, while Marie—like some others—was consigned to an "ever so brief" and "sideline" role, like those others, she "never harmed any picture."

Insight was a very special television series. It was put on by a Roman Catholic production company called Paulist Productions. The episodes were not usually specifically Catholic but dealt with moral issues from a Christian perspective. It was an anthology series with episodes ranging in genre from realistic drama to comedy to fantasy. Father Ellwood E. "Bud" Kiesser, the founder of Paulist Productions, created the concept for the show. Marie acted in an episode that aired in 1965 entitled "Bourbon in Suburbia." She played Dorothy, a middle-class housewife who believes herself a social drinker but whose concerned family knows she is sliding into alcoholism.

Marie played a brothel madam in the 1966 motion picture *Chamber of Horrors*. She later said in an interview that this film was "made from a TV pilot called *The Hook*." However, once made it was seen as not being material for living room viewing. "It was a wonderful pilot film but too gruesome for TV… no one would buy it," Marie commented.

Thus, *Chamber of Horrors* debuted in movie theaters. A horror film with a touch of the tongue-in-cheek, it clearly owes much to the Vincent Price classic *House of Wax*. It also draws on the gimmicks of director William Castle ("the poor man's Hitchcock").

Chamber of Horrors opens with truly inspired ghoulishness as anti-hero Jason Cravatte, played by Patrick O'Neal, uses a gun to persuade a minister to perform a most unusual wedding. Jason marries a freshly murdered female corpse! The grotesquerie sets the tone for what follows. Directed by Hy Averback, with a screenplay by Stephen Kandel, the story is set in the 19th Century. Jason Cravatte murdered the woman he loved upon discovering that she was not quite as "pure" as he had been led to believe. Not one to let the lack of a pulse limit his goals, he then insists on the previously described wedding.

Arrested, tried, and sentenced to hang, the wily Cravatte manages to escape on the way to his date with the executioner—but must cut off his hand to do so. Equipped with a hook in place of one hand, he sets out to avenge himself against those he believes wronged him. Reviewer Glenn Erickson observes, "Hy Averback's direction is split between fairly bland TV coverage and scenes designed with much more care and style." Much of the action takes place in a wax museum. The gimmicks are a noise said to be a "Fear Flasher" and "Horror Horn" drenching the film in red prior to the "scariest" scenes. Marie's part is that of a brothel madam who is more interested in the money she can get from the maddened scion of a fine family than in little matters like murder and mutilation.

Batman 2-parter

23

IN 1966, MARIE APPEARED in a two-parter in the classically campy
TV show *Batman*. The series was inspired by the Batman superhero created in 1939 by writer Bill Finger and artist Bob Kane. Unlike other superheroes such as Superman, Batman has no supernatural powers but
fights evildoers with a combination of wily intelligence and superb fighting skills together with the state-of-the-art technologies afforded by great
wealth. Batman is the "superhero" name of a rich fellow named Bruce
Wayne who transforms himself into "Batman" via his caped disguise. He
is accompanied by his ward Robin who becomes Boy Wonder when he
takes on *his* costume. The duo battle crime in a colorful "Gotham City"
that is a cartoon version of New York City.

The television series boasted an array of flamboyantly colorful characters on both the virtuous and vicious sides. Batman/Bruce Wayne was
played by Adam West while sidekick Robin the Boy Wonder/Dick Grayson was played by Burt Ward. In their Bruce Wayne and Dick Grayson
personas, the latter is the former's teenaged ward.

"Green Ice" and "Deep Freeze" were the names of the two-parter
episodes in which Marie appeared. The villain was Mister Freeze, played
in this episodes by famous director Otto Preminger. Mister Freeze has
launched an "Operation Hate Batman" campaign in which he aims to
sully the reputation of the caped crusader by planting false evidence that
Batman accepted bribes and by decking his own minions out as Batman
and Boy Wonder. He also aims to turn the duo into "Frosty Freezes."

Mister Freeze also has a more personal goal. He wants to marry so he
kidnaps Miss Iceland (!) (Dee Hartford) to make her his bride.

The episodes are a lot of high-spirited and creative fun. Marie plays one of the more realistic characters, a reporter named Nellie Majors. "Why can't we find out what happened?" challenges Nellie Majors, her hair in a teased mini-bouffant of a sort popular in the 1960s, at a press conference. "Commissioner Gordan and Chief O'Hara nearly freeze to death in this office on the hottest day of the year and nobody can or will give us any details whatsoever," she points out.

Batman says, "Gentlemen of the press—and this attractive young lady." Since this is the mid-1960s, reporter Majors is the one female at the event. Although Marie turned 47 years old in 1966, "attractive young lady" was not sarcastic as she retained considerable beauty.

When Batman gives her that flattering recognition, she identifies herself as Nellie Majors of the *Gotham City Herald*. She then inquires, "And might this have something to do with the kidnapping of Miss Iceland today? And might it involve a certain arch-criminal who escaped from the state penitentiary last week in an ice cream truck?" Nellie Majors wonders aloud if Batman is "on a spot" and notes that she "has seen many heroes tarnished in the course of my career." A commentator on popular culture, "Irving's Zoo," wittily observed on a website review that her fellow reporters may go along with her "because she has boobs and they don't."

In another scene, Bruce Wayne and Dick Grayson are dressed in their "regular" formal clothes and at a party given by a socialite. When Bruce notes the appearance of emeralds, Dick observes that these gems are known as "green ice" among criminals. Mister Freeze shows up. Aunt Harriet wishes aloud, "If only Batman and Robin were here!" Mister Freeze's minions show up dressed in the caped crusader costumes—and are easily bested! The witnesses are soon disappointed when the supposed heroes are exposed as inept klutzes. In another scene, Mister Freeze reminds the dynamic duo that the newspapers have run articles showing them as ineffectual fools and remarks on the "fickle" nature of the public. The episode ends on a huge question mark as Batman and Boy Wonder are shoved into gigantic "Frosty Freezes."

The next episode is "Deep Freeze." The show must go on so the extraordinary pair manage to escape. Once freed, they find a newspaper that has run an article that, as Boy Wonder observes, is a "holy distortion!" It "sure makes you look bad, Batman," Robin continues.

Yes, the reporters of Gotham City, including Nellie Majors, are writing negative depictions of the formerly beloved crime fighters and stirring public opinion against them. A little boy (Mike Durkin) walks by a store window and sees a large cutout of Batman and the Boy Wonder. "Boo, Batman," the child says and walks on—right past Bruce Wayne and Dick Grayson. Bruce comments that "nothing has cut me so deeply to the quick" as that child's "boo." The evil Mister Freeze tries to extort $1 billion by tomorrow or he will freeze Gotham City in ice.

The "real" Batman and Boy Wonder know they are still the best crime fighters and they set out to rescue Gotham City. Mister Freeze is astonished: "You were supposed to be a famous frosty freezy by now!" Batman and Boy Wonder see that he has "frozen" Miss Iceland although she can still plead for deliverance. Needless to say, the caped crusaders find a way to save themselves, save the city—and regain their reputations. Batman runs into the little boy who said "boo" when walking by the large cutouts of the caped crusader. This time, the child says, "Batman, you're the greatest." All is well in Gotham City and, presumably, Nellie Majors realizes that the tarnish is off these superheroes.

A *Bonanza* episode that aired in May 1966, "Five Sundowns to Sunup," had Marie playing a character at once mightily maternal and ruthlessly murderous. She is cast as Ma Lassiter, whose son Henry is scheduled to hang for murder. A gunslinger as experienced as Belle Starr, Ma Lassiter threatens to kidnap and murder five leading citizens in the area unless her beloved son is let out of jail without getting his neck stretched. During the tense episode, Ma and other Lassiters terrify the Cartwrights by kidnapping Little Joe and holding him hostage, even as they threaten to take more unless the condemned Henry Lassiter is returned to his loving family.

Family Time

24

EVEN AS MARIE WORKED steadily in film and TV, she found time and energy for other things. Far from being consumed by her career, she lived a well-rounded life with varied interests including a strong sense of domesticity.

During Richard's Hupp's childhood in the 1960s and 1970s, he was impressed by the energy his mother could muster and her time management skills. "She wanted to do it all—actress, artist, mom," Rick Hupp told the author of this book. "She was a very industrious woman. She was always doing something either away from the house or at home."

Mealtime was family time at the Hupp house. It was also when Marie's domesticity was most prominent. "Supper was important to her," Hupp recalls. "She made a consistent effort to have a meal on the table by the time Dad got home. She wanted to be first hand in the kitchen. The food might not be something fancy but she always put the meal together for the family. She took it seriously."

Marie was always careful to ensure that her private life received appropriate attention. "My personal happiness is much more important than my career," she stated. "My primary aim is to have a happy home life." She noted that this was not true of all actresses and that some who were successful as performers failed to enjoy a fulfilling private life, often because their time and energy was completely swallowed up by the demands of acting. "Those great ladies of the silver screen have wanted what I've been able to get but they've not been able to give up enough to get it," she speculated. She told people that having older stepson Chris around was helpful in raising little Rick.

As might be expected of one who was such an animal lover, pets were a part of Marie's life. "When I was little, we had a beagle named Freckles and a basset hound named Jasmine," Rick Hupp told this author. "Then we got a stray that we adopted, a German Shepherd and Labrador mix we named Domingo. We called him Mingo for short. Then we picked up a stray we named Bitzy. She was a mutt with terrier overtones." They also had an orange tabby named Charlie Brown and a little black cat named Mia.

The family also had a most unconventional pet obtained through an odd happenstance. "I was five or six and my Dad was washing down the driveway," Rick Hupp recalled. "Dad saw what looked like a clump of leaves. But it was a baby owl! It obviously couldn't care for itself so Dad brought it into the house. Mom called the vet who gave her ideas of what to do to keep the owl alive. The vet told her where to get nutrients and she fed the baby owl with an eyedropper." Under the ministrations of Marie and other family members, the baby owl grew into a full-fledged adult owl. "He had the run of the house," Rick Hupp disclosed. "We got a little play mouse and he zoomed in on it." The owl was named Hooty. However, during a family vacation, the person who was house-sitting accidentally allowed the owl to fly away. The family had feared that Hooty would not be equipped to fend for himself in freedom. "Sometimes we heard an owl hoot in the canyons and we hoped it was him," Rick said. "We hoped it meant he had been able to live after he left us."

Mom's Breast Cancer, Chris's Mental Illness

IN THE LATE 1960S, Marie felt her world turn upside down as terror invaded it in the form of a lump on her breast. A doctor told her that it was indeed cancerous and life-threatening. She required a double mastectomy.

Only a small child when his mother was diagnosed with an illness that could take her life as well as disfigure her, Rick Hupp remembers, "My dad was usually very stoic about things and this was no exception. My parents did not discuss much about what was going on." But there was no concealing from the child the fact that Marie required medical treatments: "I remember being scared that my mother was so bandaged up and had to be in bed."

The cancer had apparently spread to both breasts so Marie underwent a double mastectomy. "It was scary for me as a child because I didn't understand what was happening, but my mom was able to recover fairly well," Rick Hupp said. "She would have recovered faster if she had not smoked but she was tough and made it through somehow." Marie wore prosthetics under her clothes for many years to disguise the fact that she had no breasts." She did this until the 1970s. "When reconstructive surgery became more common and more reliable, she pursued it," he adds.

By this time, step-brother Chris Hupp was largely out of the Hupp household picture. "He was drafted for the Vietnam War at age 20 in 1966 and got out in 1968," Rick Hupp discloses. "I don't remember seeing much of him ever [at that time] because he lived with his mom, dad's former wife." Rick believes that the close relationship between Chris and his mother was not beneficial to him due to his mom's emotional troubles. "She was mentally unstable and, as a result, when Chris returned [from Vietnam] to the anti-war sentiment, at the time, it caused a psychological break for him." There was psychiatric help for Chris Hupp. "He got help at UCLA, and was able to become somewhat productive, but never quite independent," Rick Hupp explains. "His mom and he lived off his income and my father's alimony payments." Despite Chris Hupp's mental deterioration, he was able for awhile to engage in paid employment. "Chris had a retail job that I recall was in a store that sold nuts and gift baskets of treats," Rick discloses. "He also worked [for awhile] at the AAA auto club. And I do believe he was a mail carrier at one point. Not much else. He would eventually become unemployable due to his attitude and to alcohol." There was an incident in which Chris Hupp got a series of parking tickets but was either unwilling or unable to pay them. "I remember my dad became upset when Chris's car was impounded due to numerous unpaid parking tickets," Rick comments. "One day the car just stopped working because Chris ignored a low oil warning light." After the troubled adult Chris moved back in with his biological mother, they shared the residence for the rest of her life. "They lived together until she died, and then he took over the apartment they were staying in," Rick states. "Over time he became more and more reclusive."

Jack Hupp and Marie Windsor reached out to the deteriorating man. "He descended further and further into mental illness, and my parents supported him somewhat by paying his rent, and attempting to get him help from the VA, and making up for what Social Security couldn't cover." It is in the nature of some mental illnesses to lead the sufferer to be reluctant to accept help and, sadly, Chris was in this category. "He would not attend VA meetings and eventually became a shut-in."

According to Rick Hupp, Jack Hupp and Marie did not know how to effectively assist Chris. "My parents did not know what to do," he says. "Mom was always the compassionate one: she would send him money and try to help him despite my father's frustration. My dad preferred to cut him off but my mom recognized that Chris suffered from insensitive treatment during his childhood so she tried to offer Chris support emotionally wand financially. Eventually, she was unable to do much for him."

Guns and Glory

26

1971 SAW THE RELEASE of a motion picture in which Marie appeared that was entitled *Support Your Local Gunfighter*. It bore a strong resemblance to the earlier *Support Your Local Sheriff* in characters and plot elements but was not a sequel. The color motion picture was directed by Burt Kennedy; its screen writer was James Edward Grant. The movie was a Western comedy. James Garner starred as Latigo Smith and Suzanne Pleshette played the short-tempered and ironically named Patience. When the story opens, we see Latigo on a train with Marie's character, the loud and brassy red-haired Goldie. A wealthy woman, Goldie badly wants to marry Latigo but he is not ready to walk down the aisle—so he sneaks off the train. Then he is in the small mining town of Purgatory. After a few colorful and violent adventures, our hero consults a town doctor about a tattoo that could potentially cause him embarrassment. On his chest is tattooed: "I Love Goldie." The humorous adventures of Latigo include difficulties caused by his compulsive gambling and being mistaken for infamous gunslinger "Swifty" Morgan. Ever a fellow to think on his feet, Latigo suggests to others that a klutzy fool named Jug May (Jack Elam) is the real Swifty Morgan, a subterfuge that explodes when the real Swifty Morgan, played by—who else?—Chuck Connors ambles into Purgatory. To add to Latigo's many woes, he finds himself embroiled in romance with saloonkeeper Miss Jenny (Joan Blondell) and Patience as well as being found once again by Goldie. The whole thing blows up quite literally as well metaphorically. Marie's Goldie is not onscreen often but, when she is, her rowdy presence adds to the picaresque atmosphere.

Marie said she was not the first choice for the role of Goldie. "I replaced Marilyn Maxwell," she revealed. "They didn't think she had the feistiness the part required." It troubled Marie to know that the other actress must have suffered disappointment when her interpretation of the role was found wanting. "I felt badly about it," she said. "Marilyn and I had known each other since the early 1940s." Additionally, Marilyn Maxwell had played in the 1970 TV film *Wild Women* with Marie. *Support Your Local Gunfighter* has a distinction no other Marie Windsor vehicle boasts: it is the only motion picture in which Marie wore a wig. "I ended up wearing the red wig [Marilyn Maxwell] was supposed to wear."

However, the 1970s found Marie on the small screen much more than the big screen. She played guest roles on many TV series. Marie made a guest appearance on *Hawaii Five-O* in 1971 as madam Gloria Marshall. But Marie's madam is not a callous exploiter. Instead, she is a caring woman deeply concerned because a serial strangler is on the loose targeting ladies of the evening. The police have asked for her help and she is eager to give it. Marie plays Gloria not as a "tart with a heart" stereotype but as a normal, intelligent, and compassionate individual who happens to have a stigmatized job. She visits former "working girl" Cathy Field (Sheila Wells) to let her know that cops believe the man is pursuing her—or a kind of image of her—and to urge her to help police find the murderer. But Cathy is resistant because she fears endangering her marriage to Henry Fields (Norman Dupont) who is unaware of her past.

The early 1970s saw Marie play on three episodes of the popular police series *Adam-12*. In a 1972 episode entitled "The Chaser," Marie played observant diner waitress Jenny who alerts officers Pete Malloy (Martin Milner) and Jim Reed (Kent McCord) that a restaurant patron has a gun on him.

Marie played a major part in a 1970 made-for-TV movie entitled *Wild Women*. Lou Morheim and Richard Carr co-wrote a teleplay based on Vincent Fotre's novel *The Trailmakers*. Don Taylor directed *Wild Women*. The flick opens with a group of women gathered outdoors and around a pair of women who are having a knockdown drag out fight. The women around are cheering on the brutal fight. Proceedings are brought to an abrupt halt with the arrival of a group of men.

The women are prisoners in a stockade. A man named Killian (Hugh O'Brian) is trying to smuggle firearms into Texas at the time of the Texas Revolution. He needs help to do this and wants the men under his command to pass for a group of settlers. Thus, they need fake "wives" to make it seem like such a group. Marie plays Lottie Clampett. It is never said, but seems possible to this writer, that she is meant to suggest an ancestress or at least relative of *The Beverly Hillbillies* Clampetts. Other women playing women inmates inducted to play faux wives include Anne Frances, Marilyn Maxwell, Sherry Jackson, and Cynthia Hull. As they are on their way, they naturally run into obstacles such as Indians offended at the use of a pond they regard as their own and some Mexican soldiers who suspect the true purpose of the "settlers." As might be expected of the film, the female inmates have trouble adjusting to "normal" life but eventually rise to the occasion—including Marie's loud, brash, and brassy Lottie.

Marie played Louella, a small supporting part, in a 1971 Western entitled *One More Train To Rob*. The film had a screenplay by Don Tait and Dick Nelson and was directed by Andrew McLaglen. It is about train robber Harker Fleet (George Peppard) who takes the fall for his crime partners and seeks vengeance when he gets out of the pokey.

Alias Smith and Jones, a TV Western series, aired in 1972 the episode "High Lonesome Country" in which Marie appeared. The show itself was based on the concept that two outlaw cousins, Hannibal Heyes and Jedediah "Kid" Curry, wanted to reform. The governor gave them a clemency deal with two conditions: the agreement must be kept secret, and they had to live as wanted fugitives until the governor considered the time right for a public and formal amnesty. Until officially pardoned, they would use the names Thaddeus Jones and Joshua Smith.

In "High Lonesome Country," Kid Curry/Thaddeus Jones (Ben Murphy) and Hannibal Heyes/Joshua Smith (Roger Jones) are in a saloon when they make the acquaintance of rancher Phil Archer (Buddy Ebsen). "Smith" and "Jones" identify themselves as trapper and the rancher reveals he has been looking for trappers.

Phil and the guys he has hired to do trapping on his land enjoy a meal with, and prepared by, the rancher's wife, Helen Archer, who is played by Marie. When our heroes are not in sight, Helen reveals to Phil, "One of those guys is Kid Curry." It obviously follows that the other is Hannibal Heyes. Phil Archer knows there is a bounty on those outlaws and resolves to collect. However, Phil is not the best bounty hunter so he enlists the aid of a well-known bounty hunter who tells Phil he does not want the job. It becomes evident that he just does not wish to divide up the award money. As is typical for a Western, there is a lot of shooting back and forth with all our major characters endangered by the bullets whizzing around them. Marie's Helen starts out traditionally domestic, serving food for the men before confiding her pivotal conclusions to her husband. As the plot heats up, Helen Archer's skills with firearms and on the saddle are put on display. It is likely that, yet again, Marie's experiences as a horsewoman helped get her a part.

"Mystery of the Green Feather" was the intriguing title of a 1972 *Hec Ramsey* series in which Marie appeared. *Hec Ramsey* was a TV series in which Richard Boone starred as the title character. A Western set in the early 20th century, producer Jack Webb, who shot to glory in the TV crime series *Dragnet*, called *Hec Ramsey* "*Dragnet* meets John Wayne." Toward the start of the episode, law officers Hec and Chief Oliver Stamp (Rick Lenz) saunter into a hotel where we find Marie playing Madame Irma. Decked out in a glamorous outfit accented with a pink feather boa, this proprietor informs the law officers that the fellow they seek is indeed in the hotel. "He's waiting for you," she explains. "He's tired of running." She adds, "I hate him!" Asked why, she replies, "I've got linen sheets and that varmint wouldn't take his boots off!" Hec and Chief leave Madame Irma behind and she is not seen again in this episode.

"Twenty Million Alibis" was the title of a 1973 *Barnaby Jones* episode in which Marie played wealthy burglary victim Carole Morrison whose super-valuable necklace was stolen. The burglary turned into a murder because the Morrison butler happened to be at the residence when sticky fingers grabbed it. The reason for the episode's title? Barnaby suspects the perpetrator was supposedly retired burglar turned author Tony Neill (Peter Haskell) who was seen on a TV talk show with twenty million viewers at the time of the crime.

Marie had a supporting role in a Western film released in 1973 that starred John Wayne. *Cahill U. S. Marshal* was the fourth, and last, vehicle she would share with the Duke. Rita M. Fink and Harry Julian Fink co-wrote the screenplay based on a story by Barney Slater and Andrew V. McLaglen directed the movie. While Wayne's character, Marshal J. D. Cahill is away on a call of duty, teenaged son Danny (Gary Grimes) and pre-teen son Billy (Clay O'Brien) gets into mischief. Or more accurately, the kids get into genuinely heavy crime as they help an outlaw gang headed by Abe Fraser (George Kennedy) escape from jail and then rob a bank! Needless to say, things are pretty bad when a boy not even in his teens helps commit a bank robbery. What's more, the bank robbery went wrong—very wrong—as a town sheriff is murdered during the heist.

Little Billy hides the loot while big brother plus the gang return to their jail cells (yes, teenager Danny has seen the inside of the pokey) to secure an alibi.

Marshal Cahill returns home. He enlists Danny and "half-breed" tracker Lightfoot (Neville Brand) to search for the bank robbers-cum-murderers (the lawman not suspecting his own kids could have done such a thing). Marshal Cahill arrests four suspects even though he suspects they might have just been in the wrong place at the wrong time. Despite his suspicions, a jury convicts and a judge sentences the four to death. Will the truth come out? Will four innocent men hang? What led the children of a U. S. Marshal to get so deeply into crime? Working out these questions is the focus of the film.

Writing for *The New York Times*, Vincent Canby noted a problem in the film: the hero's age. John Wayne was 66 when he made the film. Of course, males can sire children when they are one hundred years old, but Wayne would look to most observers like "Grandpa" rather than "Dad" to two youngsters. Canby writes that it "has become increasingly difficult to accept" the aging actor's "peculiar physical presence" as he seems to be "swelling up like a balloon." When he "gets shot several times, and stabbed once" his easy healing makes him seem "a plastic man." Canby found the movie "a tacky Western of drowsy pace" but elaborated that, perhaps out of awareness of Wayne's age-imposed limitations, they try "to turn a conventional Western into a children-in-peril movie." A critic at a website called *At-A-Glance Film Reviews* called the movie "pedestrian" but acknowledged "some clever and entertaining touches" as well as saying that John Wayne "shows the human side to his character more than usual." This author agrees with those observations. One "clever and entertaining touch" has Marshal Cahill unable to get a horse so he tries to ride a rambunctious donkey! One presumes a (much younger) stuntman took over this part. There are also touching scenes when the boys talk about how they feel neglected by their Dad who says, "Even grown men need understanding."

Marie's character is met when the film is about one-fifth of the way through. She is Mrs. Green of "Mrs. Green's Boarding House." Mrs. Green displays maternal affection to Billy, saying, "It'll be nice to have a young boy around." There is a suggestion that she has romantic desires for the Marshal when she adds, "If he stays, it'll be the first Cahill I've been able to keep under my roof." Mrs. Green is not on much but she is appropriately comforting and warm with the youngsters, friendly and a touch flirtatious with their Pa.

During the making of *Cahill U. S. Marshal* Marie found a "distasteful" aspect to the environment. "This film was shot in Durango, Mexico," she remarked. "The food was lousy! You would look out the dining room window and see a lamb tied to a stake. You knew what you would have for dinner and you didn't like it!" She further revealed that an uncharacteristic absentmindedness on Marie's part led to a scene having to be re-shot. "There's a shot where I'm driving a wagon with two children," she recalled. "The long shot picks up at a distance from the house as we come down a hill. We got halfway down the hill when Andy McLaglen yelled, 'Cut! Marie, take off those damn sunglasses!'"

Making *Cahill U. S. Marshal* required Marie to spend time away from the "men in her life"—husband Jack Hupp and son Rick Hupp—which she did not like to do. An article published in the *Lubbock Avalanche-Journal* noted that she had been on location for the film for "five weeks—the longest she has ever been away from her family." She praised her husband Jack Hupp for helping her put family first. "Jack has always been wonderful, very understanding, because his father was the silent actor Earl Rodney," she commented. That same article discussed her basic approach to life. "I've never been discouraged," she asserted. "I've always believed that something good is coming around the corner." The article was illustrated by a photograph of Marie holding the hand of son Rick who was ten years old at the time. As previously noted, Marie was a true actress, changing affect as the part required. She told the *Lubbock Avalanche-Journal* that she followed what a script required: "I'll do anything a part requires. If they say they want purple hair, I'll dye my hair purple. I'm not temperamental about anything if they wave work in front of my eyes!" At the time the piece was written, Marie and her family resided in what the reporter described as "a modest, ranch-style house in a Hollywood Hills canyon."

In another 1973 film, a contemporary action movie called *The Outfit*, Marie had a bit part. *The Outfit* starred Robert Duvall, Karen Black, Joe Don Baker, and Robert Ryan. Characteristic of its genre, it was filled with unsavory characters and plenty of fists flying and guns blazing. Marie's character, a woman named Madge, is only in a single scene where she looks jaded and world weary. She is seen behind a bar, making streetwise remarks like "They'll kick your ass." She compliments Karen Black's Brett Harrow for being "real nice-looking" but notes that a fellow under discussion "never worked with a woman" for long. Duvall's Earl Macklin dryly notes, "Time's change." Interestingly, Sheree North, whose heyday as a Marilyn Monroe wannabe was in the 1950s and 1960s, also had a bit part in this flick. Although pushing forty, North still looks enough the sexpot for the audience to wonder about it when Jack Cody (Joe Don Baker) turns down the goods she offers.

Marie played a bit part in a 1974 made-for-TV pilot, *The Manhunter,* for a short-lived TV show of the same title. *The Manhunter* starred Ken Howard and Stephanie Powers. Set in America in the 1930s, it is about a man searching for the "Clinger Gang" of bank robbers and murderers. The group appears to be modeled after the "Barrow Gang" of Bonnie and Clyde fame since there is a lady alongside bandit Frank Clinger. Ken Howard plays good guy/"manhunter" Dave Barrett, Gary Lockwood is Frank Clinger, and Stephanie Powers is Clinger's girlfriend/crime partner Ann Louise Hovis. Marie's bit is as May of "May's Place," a boardinghouse and brothel combo. She is appropriately blowsy, frowzy, and loud as she hollers her flamboyantly friendly, "Welcome to fun town" at Dave when she believes he is there for "some company."

1974 also saw Marie go through a major change in her appearance. "I believe she had her first facelift in 1974," Rick Hupp informed this author. Does Rick believe that cosmetic surgery operation actually improved his mother's appearance? "Yes," he replied. "When I look at older actresses today, they have an attractive face that still looks like them, but you can tell something has shifted. The way they appear, you know something has changed, but you can't quite tell what. That's what I remember about my mom."

Hearts of the West is the title of a 1975 movie in which Marie appeared. The flick zigzags between Western and a movie-about-the-movies. Set in the 1930s, it focuses on a young man, Lewis Tater (Jeff Bridges), who wants to write Westerns. In particular, he wants to be like the famous author of Westerns, Zane Grey.

Our ambitious Zane Grey-wannabe enrolls in a correspondence school for aspiring writers called the University of Titan. He heads to Titan, Nevada in hopes of actually attending the school, not realizing that it does not really exist. By happy accident, he stumbles—quite literally—into a Western film being made by Tumbleweed Productions. He becomes especially impressed by cowboy-actor Howard Pike (Andy Griffith). Tumbleweed executive Bert Kessler (Alan Arkin) hires Lewis. The film's production manager, Miss Trout (Blythe Danner) attracts Lewis. In his writing aspirations, he switches from Zane to a (fictional) Western writer named Billy Pueblo. There are several more plot ups and downs, some involving the crooks who ran the fake correspondence school. Respected film critic Roger Ebert praised *Hearts of the West* as a "lovely little comedy" and applauds Jeff Bridges for bringing "a nice complexity to the role." Equally respected movie reviewer Vincent Candy called it a "benign comedy" that is "carried by the consistent intelligence of its observations and the sweetness with which it tolerates ineffectual rogues, rascals and fanatics of a very parochial kind."

Marie has a bit part early in *Hearts of the West*. She seems to be managing a hotel although she is credited only as "Woman In Nevada." Given the 1930s setting, it seems odd the makers of the film did not give her a bigger role and/or make any allusion to her glory days. However, as noted, whether film, TV show, or stage, Marie could always be depended upon to correctly fill a part.

Aging Gracefully, Having Fun

Marie starred in a 1976 made-for-TV movie called *Stranded* about a group of airline passengers struggling to survive on an island after their plane crashes. She plays alongside Kevin Dobson, Lara Parker of *Dark Shadows* fame, Devon Ericson, Jimmy McNichol, and others. Unfortunately, this writer could neither see the film nor find out much information about it.

Released in theaters in 1976 was a spiky Disney movie entitled *Freaky Friday* in which Marie put in a brief appearance. *Freaky Friday* is a fantasy-comedy in which a middle-class mother and her 13-year-old daughter miraculously inhabit each other's bodies for a day (a Friday in case the title failed to inform anyone). Jodie Foster played teenager Annabel Andrews, Barbara played mother Ellen Andrews, and John Astin played father Bill Andrews. Marie was in a single scene as brisk and authoritative typing teacher Mrs. Murphy who suffers quite a shock when the "possessed by an adult" kid causes a classroom full of electricity to short circuit. "Shock" is an all-too-correct word!

In 1979 Marie appeared in a *Fantasy Island* episode entitled "Séance/The Treasure." Her character was pivotal in the "Séance" section as she played a medium named Madame Estelle Vorick. Madame Vorick is trying to help grieving Clare Conti (Eve Plumb) communicate with her deceased brother. He is believed to have committed suicide about a year previously… or was his death something else? Marie plays Madame Vorick in a dignified manner that suggests a true believer rather than a flamboyant fraud. She seems utterly sincere when she conducts the séances and when she declares, "If you're not a believer, you have no place here!" As an IMDb reviewer states, Marie gives a "solid performance."

Also in 1979, Marie found herself reunited with Elisha Cook, Jr. with whom she had done such powerful work in Stanley Kubrick's *The Killing*. "It's so great to work with you again," Elisha Cook, Jr. said as he handed Marie a lovely box. She opened it to find a big and beautiful orchid inside. The project that reunited this pair was *Salem's Lot*, a 1979 made-for-TV mini-series. *Salem's Lot* producer Richard Kobritz wanted the two actors cast in a relationship in the program because he is a Stanley Kubrick fan. This mini-series was a relatively faithful adaptation of the Stephen King novel of the same name and has become a cult film. Tobe Hooper, best known for *The Texas Chain Saw Massacre* (1974), directed it. Paul Monash wrote the screenplay.

The *Salem's Lot* mini-series starts in Ximico, Guatemala with Ben Mears (David Soul) and Mark Petrie (Lance Kerwin) filling small bottles with holy water. An odd flashing comes off a bottle. "They've found us!" Mears realizes.

We are transported two years before to events in the small town of Salem's Lot, Maine. The town's title is eerie as it echoes the infamous witch trials held in Salem, Massachusetts.

Ben Mears is a successful author—Stephen King is drawn to protagonists who, like himself, are successful authors—who has returned to his hometown of Salem's Lot after being away for a long time. He wants to write about the Marsten House, a building with a history of evil doings that include murders both known and suspected and a reputation as being haunted. Naturally enough, he wishes to rent the house so he can research its bad reputation. He learns it is being rented by someone else who has recently arrived in the town, Richard Straker (James Mason). It is suggested he find lodgings at the boarding house run by Eva Miller, who is played by Marie.

Ben reconnects with old acquaintances and stirs a romance with townswoman Susan Norton. As he is finding old friends and making new ones, Constable Parkins Gillespie (Kenneth McMillan) meets up with a seedy, sloppily dressed old fellow who is drinking booze straight out of a bottle still encased in a brown paper bag—something that shouts "street bum" as loudly as anything could. This individual is Gordon "Weasel" Phillips who is played by Elisha Cook Jr. The cop asks Weasel to keep an eye on Ben Mears. Although Weasel is perplexed by the request, he agrees to do so. Other characters eventually inform us that Eva Miller and Weasel were once married. Although they are now divorced, their estrangement is incomplete as Weasel lives at Eva's boardinghouse. Still another character informs us that in the not-too-distant past, Eva was "quite a dish." The more mature Eva is far from unattractive.

Wanting to be true to his promise to the chief law enforcement official in Salem's Lot, Weasel sneaks into Mears's room to find a paper at his typewriter describing the Marsten House as "the essence of evil." Eva finds him poking around and is less angry with her ex-husband than impressed by the way her new tenant can turn a phrase.

It turns out that Salem's Lot has become infested with thirsty vampires and the small town is soon in danger of becoming Salem's Vampire Village—unless our hero, Ben Mears, assisted by teenager Mark Petrie, can do something to stop the unification of the town under the undead.

Marie is seen only a few times and always quite briefly. However, her last scene in the film puts up a tantalizing possibility. She recounts the previous night's slumber: "I had such a sweet dream. Weasel and I were young, just like old times, and he was kissing me on the neck." The implications are left unresolved as the film moves on.

Salem's Lot was a special treat for Marie specifically because it reunited her with Elisha Cook, Jr. "Elisha was a real character," she commented. "He was pleasantly off-the-wall, full of energy." What's more, she continued, "He brought me a white orchid with a sweet note about how happy he was about our reunion."

As the Queen of the Bs moved beyond middle age and into "seasoned citizen" status, she sometimes took parts that played on her quasi-*Sunset Boulevard* status. I write "quasi" because Marie was never a "has-been" pining for her younger years. Unlike the fictional Norma Desmond—and all-too-many real life performers—her career had not vanished when she was no longer young. Rather, the skillful Marie Windsor gracefully aged into mature parts and supporting roles.

Charlie's Angels, with its trio of drop-dead gorgeous young female detectives, was a phenomenon of the 1970s. Marie acted in two episodes on the show, one that aired in 1978 and the other in 1979. First episode is "Angels in Springtime" in which she appears as aged actress Eve Le Deux. She is glamorous in her pink outfit as she gets ready to relax in a hot tub at a spa. Oops! Eve Le Deux is soon electrocuted. Learning it was probably not an accident, Charlie's Angels are on the case. "Angels at the Altar" has Marie play the upper-class mother-of-the-bride.

In two *Lou Grant* episodes, Marie was cast into stories that alluded to her film noir heyday. The first such episode was entitled "Hollywood" and aired in 1979 while the second was called "Libel" and aired in 1980.

"Hollywood" had the newsroom investigating a cold case from the film noir era. The structure took on the air of a classic Hollywood mystery by having the episode begin with Lou doing a voiceover to set up the story to the wail of a saxophone. The journalists look into the 1940s murder of a boxer who was popular with the film crowd. Besides Marie, other Hollywood old timers in "Hollywood" include Margaret Hamilton, John Larch, Laraine Day, Nina Foch, and Howard Duff.

In this *Lou Grant* episode, Marie is not an aging movie star. Instead, she is a tailor who sews costumes for entertainment big shots. As befits a woman who devotes herself to creating costumes, Marie appears to us richly decked out in colorful garb, so colorful that another character mistakes her for a "Gypsy."

The 1980 *Lou Grant* episode in which Marie has a supporting role is entitled "Libel." This episode was clearly inspired by the Jean Seberg tragedy. That incident occurred in the 1970s when the FBI was using a variety of dirty tricks to undermine the black power movement. Actress Seberg had been a supporter of the Black Panthers. When she was pregnant, gossip columnist Joyce Haber published a column in the respected newspaper *The Los Angeles Times*, entitled "An Apple for Miss A" in which she discussed a pregnant actress who had been impregnated "by a prominent Black Panther." Seberg was not mentioned by name but, to those familiar with her life and career, it was obviously about her.

Seberg was white as was her husband—by whom she was pregnant. Apparently she got so upset at the accusation that she was pregnant through adultery that it contributed to a miscarriage.

In "Libel," a tabloid called the *National Spectator* publishes an article saying a pregnant actress had been impregnated through an extramarital affair instead of by her husband. As with Seberg, the actress miscarries.

There are two major manners in which the *Lou Grant* case breaks with its inspiration. First, there is no racial/political element. Second, the publication that publishes the false story is a tabloid rather than a respected newspaper like the *L.A. Times*. Indeed, the title is obviously meant to resemble *The National Enquirer*.

Lou decides his newspaper will run a piece revealing the nasty, and often downright false, orientation of *The National Spectator*.

Reporter Billie Newsome is dispatched to interview an aged actress who was also victimized by a false and unkind article. She is Janet Hart, played by Marie, who is suing *The National Spectator* for running a piece stating that Hart had been a hooker in her younger years. There is a kind of reverse parallel between the situation of Janet Hart and that of Marie Windsor. Marie's sensitivity toward others and commitment to "The Golden Rule" contrasted sharply with the violence and heartlessness of some of the characters she played. Janet Hart played a wholesome mother-figure in a show but was falsely accused of having once been a "lady of the evening" in a scandal rag.

Janet Hart had filed a lawsuit against *The National Spectator.* Lou Grant says, "Janet Hart she was in some great pictures." Billie finds Janet Hart and asks about her suit. She explains that "They say the woman who plays dear kind Molly Fletcher used to be a hooker. It makes the network nervous, the producer nervous, and me madder than hell." Janet recalls the suit was filed for her "two little granddaughters." As a dancer in Las Vegas, she lived with her mother and "didn't even kiss boys on the first date." Perhaps realizing that some 1980s readers might be taken aback by this level of sexual restraint, a smiling Janet immediately adds, "And don't print that either!"

1980 saw Marie play "Belle Starr" for the second time! The character she depicted in "Sideshow," an *Incredible Hulk* episode, was not the original Belle Starr she portrayed in *Stories of the Century* but a carnival worker who adopted Belle Starr as a stage name. *The Incredible Hulk*, of course, was a modern science fiction TV series inspired, at least to some extent, by the Robert Louis Stevenson classic *Dr. Jekyll and Mr. Hyde.* In the show, scientist Dr. David Banner performed an experiment that leads him to grow into a creature of enormous size and strength when angered or outraged. David Banner was played by Bill Bixby and the "Hulk" alter ego was played by Lou Ferrigno.

"Sideshow" was not only the second time Marie played a character named Belle Starr but the second time she played a carnival worker. The episode revolves around a "psychic" who travels with Belle Starr and is believed jinxed. The psychic, Nancy (Judith Chapman), was involved in a death that led some to believe she is under a curse. The dead man's father, Mr. Benedict (Robert Donner), stalks Nancy. The episode begins with Belle Starr hearkening back to her namesake: she fires a warning shot at David and snarls, "Get away from her!" in the mistaken belief he is an attacker. She learns his benign intentions and profusely apologizes. The episode is, overall, a satisfactory *Incredible Hulk* episode. One IMDb reviewer commented, "Different locale this time is a nice change; otherwise this is acceptable if unremarkable." Another reviewer found the episode "eerily prophetic" when the viewer watches "Bill Bixby listening to Donner talk about how it feels to have a child die" when Bixby in real life would suffer "this very tragedy with his own son." A third IMDb reviewer found the plot "captivating."

Home and Holidays

28

AS PREVIOUSLY NOTED, Marie strived mightily to balance her work outside the home with her personal life. Interviewed by this author, her son Rick Hupp recalled that major holidays—especially the end of the year "Big 3"—were well observed in his household.

Marie's creative bent was especially helpful in making for fun Halloweens. "Mom took great delight in building costumes out of papier-mâché," he fondly remembers. "She could make a head the size of a big beach ball and designed it as a character or animal. She built me a costume like an owl and one like a dragon. One year she made me a costume of a big wriggle worm! There was a thing like a big slinky or something you can crawl through and Mom used it to make a tail for me!"

The star's talent for cooking came in handy when Thanksgiving rolled around. "Thanksgiving was a big deal at our house because Mom liked cooking and enjoyed bringing people together," Rick Hupp stated. "She took great pride in making all the food herself. We had a traditional Thanksgiving meal: turkey, gravy, mashed potatoes, rolls, and yams." Father Jack Hupp did his part at Thanksgiving celebrations. "My Dad liked carving the turkey," Hupp explained.

Christmas meant a lot of both getting and giving at the Windsor/Hupp home. "Mom and Dad were quite popular so we would get over 100 Christmas cards," Hupp stated. "We got so many we could string them together on ribbons. We put them on those ribbons in a room and half the ceiling had cards from our friends hanging down from it!" During the year, Marie prepared for Christmas. "Mom kept lists of what people were interested in so she could get them gifts they wanted," Hupp continued. She was very conscientious in letting people know she was thinking of them." Christmas meant a small vacation from home for Jack, Marie, Chris, and Rick. "We always drove to her parents' house in Marysvale, Utah for Christmas," Hupp commented. "It was a real traditional Christmas there: cold, snowy, with freezing ice crackling under our feet. Mom and Dad went to great trouble to pack all our gifts so we could all be together. Mom and Dad always got plenty of gifts for me and Chris."

29

A "Real Pro"

AS SHE GOT WELL INTO MIDDLE AGE, opportunities for work decreased in films for theatrical release. She largely divided her time between television, including made-for-TV movies, and the stage. She most assuredly kept busy, an occasion for comment by actor and talk show host Skip E. Lowe when he interviewed her. Despite her previously noted domestic streak, she cheekily quipped, "I sometimes wonder if I don't keep busy just to avoid housework!"

Indeed, she had not acted in a film intended for theatrical release since her role in the 1975 *Hearts of the West* when she got the opportunity for a bit part in the campily entertaining, so-bad-it's-good 1981 *Lovely But Deadly*, a high-spirited combination karate/stoner/hot babes flick. It was directed by David Sheldon and with a screenplay he co-wrote with Patricia Joyce.

The "Lovely" of the film is Mary Ann Lovett (Lucinda Dooling), who prefers the nickname Lovely because, being a peppery and spirited teenager, she dislikes the innocence suggested by "Mary Ann."

After Lovely's brother is killed in an accident she attributes to the high from the illegal drugs he had been ingesting, Lovely starts her own personal War On Drugs as she sets out to pulverize into oblivion the dealers who sell the illicit substances to other high school kids. Seeming to possess karate skills surpassing *Billy Jack* caliber, she whacks around a dealer before finally shoving his own supply quite literally down his throat. There are several instances of our heroine beating holy hell out of strong males and one of an extended catfight between our Lovely and another pretty "teenaged" girl. I put "teenaged" in quotes because, as is typical of the genre, this movie had performers who were years past a normal high school graduation age playing teenagers.

Marie had a small part as Lovely's kind and caring Aunt May. This author asked *Lovely But Deadly*'s director and co-screenwriter, David Sheldon, how Marie got this part. "I needed a star to add to John Randolph and Richard Herd and our casting director recommended Marie Windsor whom I remembered as 'Queen of the B movie,'" he answered.

Although many readers may not recognize the names of John Randolph and Richard Herd, they were recognizable to audiences of the time period as they had enjoyed long careers as supporting actors.

Sheldon added that another factor in Marie's background was important to her getting a part in *Lovely But Deadly*: "When I found out that she was trained as an actress by Madam Ouspenskaya, I was sold."

The wholesomeness of the character of Aunt May might have been especially appealing to her, Sheldon says. "I was a member of the Actors Studio in New York," he reveals. "I figured she would love to play a role like Aunt May instead of another femme fatale."

What did Sheldon find her to be like as an actress? "She was a real pro," he replies. "She came to the set on time, knew her lines, and, best of all, added her own personality."

The femme fatale of so many mid-century flicks worked with a cast primarily of much younger performers on *Lovely But Deadly*. Sheldon says there was no "generation gap" problem on-set. "There was no tension at all between her and the younger actors," he asserts. "The cast looked up to her in awe and appreciated the affection she gave them. She never treated them motherly, but rather as equals. I think they learned from her."

Nothing unexpected happened behind the scenes, Sheldon elaborates. "Her appearance was smooth, no glitches of anything unexpected or funny," the director states. Of course, it had been years since her last motion picture job but Sheldon considers this to have worked as a kind of plus. "She was grateful to be working again in a film," he observes.

Also in 1981, Marie lent her considerable skills to a made-for-TV movie entitled *The Perfect Woman*. It is a science fiction comedy of deliberately ostentatious silliness. The movie started with a voiceover by Marie. "In the beginning, God created the universe and man in his image." She continues about how the deity wanted harmony and peace but wars were waged. "In a distant galaxy, a great conquering warrior" managed to change many things for the better. Named Kroger the First, he was "most powerful throughout the galaxy." Kroger the First took a special interest in the planet earth." He took his queen from a "perfect woman" from 16th Century earth and established his dynasty.

Generations passed and a council of the planet of old Kroger, the planet Zucco, sits assembled around a table. Among those assembled is Zelda, played by Marie, whose head is swathed in a bright red cap and who wears a garment flaunting super-sized sleeves. The council seeks a Queen (female) for King Kroger the Eighth. They send two of his closest aides, Zig (Peter Kastner) and Emo (Barry Gordon), to request that he find a lady with whom to carry on the dynasty. They find the king watching a TV on which he plays old black and white earth movies. He has also decorated his room with bachelor pad-style cheesecake posters. "I like being a bachelor," King Kroger (Fred Willard) informs his assistants. They impress upon him the concerns of his council. He agrees to seek a mate but on one condition: like the founder of the dynasty, the great King Kroger the First, #8 must have a "perfect woman" from planet earth. She must be beautiful, intelligent, kind, and of high morals.

The council is delighted that the king will seek a bride but not-so-delighted about his choice of planet upon which to find her. Zelda hits upon a plan to make it unlikely he can find his perfect woman among earthlings. The candidate must have a crescent-shaped beauty mark close to her breast—as did the perfect woman who wed King Kroger the First.

Zig and Emo are given all these instructions. Then they hurtle through hundreds of thousands of light-years to 1980s America. A series of "fish out of water" comic mix-ups follow but they soon find Julie (Joanne Nail), a woman who meets all the criterion—at least the ones visible when fully clothed. Can they get a glimpse of her skin under her breast without offending her or making a pass (needless to say, they dare not make advances to a prospective Queen of Zucco). They get a glimpse of Julie and whaddya know? She has a crescent-shaped beauty mark in just the right place.

Once convinced of the reality of planet Zucco, our Julie is happy to travel across the galaxy to meet her King Charming. He is eager to meet her. Unh-oh! We sense a fly in the ointment when he talks about wanting an earth woman because females from that planet are less "liberated" than those on his own.

Viewers probably expect the show to end with the wedding. It does not as Julie soon shows that she is not the subservient and submissive earth woman her king expected. She cleanses the royal bedroom of cheesecake posters and even kicks out the TV set.

Worst of all, she casts aspersions on the reproductive practice on Zucco. And here this cheesy made-for-TV movie introduces a matter to chew on. It just so happens that planet Zucco has perfected extra-uterine fetal development. Its women are pregnant very temporarily before placing the embryo in some sort of device. Julie expresses the notion that women should be able to choose whether or not they wish to bear babies. Zelda informs her the matter is "settled" on Zucco, the men of which do not like seeing pregnant bodies (unlike earth, Zucco has no pregnancy fetishists!). That explanation fails to satisfy Queen Julie the First who believes its women should "choose" whether to have their babies developed in or out of their bodies.

What makes this fictional "controversy" interesting is that one of the most famous of the second wave feminists, Shulamith Firestone, proposed in her book, *The Dialectic of Sex*, that women would finally be truly emancipated when the artificial womb was developed and perfected to the point that it is the "normal" method of having babies. *The Perfect Woman* shows us a woman rebelling against this "reality."

At any rate, our King Kroger the Eighth and Queen Julie the First manage to, as Marie tells us in the ending voiceover, "carry on the dynasty" in a "marriage filled with as many moments of happiness as it was unexpected surprises from his queen."

In 1982, Marie put in an appearance on the ever-popular TV soap opera *General Hospital* as Dr. Vivian Collins. In the 1987-1988 *General Hospital* season, Marie played Dr. Collins whose specialty was obstetrics and whose special friend was prominent character Dr. Steve Hardy.

In 1983, the motion picture community recognized Marie's accomplishments with a star on the Hollywood Walk of Fame. The star is at 1549 N. Vine St. in the Motion Pictures segment of the Walk of Fame and it was dedicated to her on January 19, 1983.

According to Rick Hupp, Marie had the second of what would eventually be three facelifts in the early 1980s. "I believe she had three of them with about seven years in between each one," Rick related to this author.

Marie played in an episode of the television series *Scarecrow and Mrs. King* that aired in 1984. Despite its title, the show was not any kind of horror or Gothic program but a spy/romance program. It starred Bruce Boxleitner as spy Lee Stetson who was code-named Scarecrow and Kate Jackson, who shot to fame in the 1970s as one of *Charlie's Angels*, as the divorced housewife Amanda King and mother of two who becomes his partner in espionage and eventually in romance. Beverly Garland, known as a blonde bombshell back when Marie was best known as a femme fatale, portrays Amanda's mother. Her feisty children are Jaime (Greg Morton) and Philip (Paul Stout). The spying is done on behalf of an organization known as "the Agency." Lee's Agency boss is the demanding Billy Melrose (Mel Stewart). A co-worker in espionage is the sprightly and lovely Francine Demond.

The episode in which Marie played was "Remembrance of Things Passed." A series of fatal attacks are made on Agency agents. Several threats are made to Lee. As a result, Lee and Billy Melrose fake Lee's death. Amanda is informed just in time to pull her out of mourning. Being officially deceased makes it possible for Lee, together with Amanda, to investigate the actual murders. Marie's character, Mrs. Peters, appears after the episode is about ¾ through and is seen in a brief scene. Mrs. Peters is a retired Agency personnel official. Lee finds her in what appears to be a retirement community. She recalls a sad story that led to a peculiar hiring. Actor Russell Sinclair (Doug McClure) was known for acting the part of espionage expert. When making a show in which he played a dashing spy, there was a terrible accident that left him badly disfigured. Unable to act, he wanted to work as an actual spy. Mrs. Peters knew he was unqualified but hired him to work at the Agency—as a janitor. She disclosed that a series of plastic surgeries had helped diminish his disfigurement. But his bitterness was not something that a surgeon's scalpel could touch.

Marie's television work during this period included a memorable stint on that anthology famed for its blending of horror and macabre humor, *Tales from the Darkside*

"If it seems too good to be true, it probably is." That old saying seems the basis for a 1985 *Tales from the Darkside* episode in which Marie played. "A New Lease on Life" is the episode's title. Archie Fenton has just moved into the St. George, a $200 a month apartment in a neighborhood in which apartments typically rent to $1,000 a month. He could not resist the good deal—we all like to regard ourselves as smart shoppers—and signed a two-year lease for this oh-so-reasonably priced apartment. Still, as he moves in, he senses there might be a catch. Does it lack a closet? A bathroom? No, they are there and in good working order. The apartment even has a nice view.

But there seems a negative omen when a St. George maintenance man drops the microwave Archie has brought and it shatters to pieces.

Just then the landlady, played by Marie, walks in. Wearing a shiny blue housecoat and big harlequin spectacles, she informs her new tenant, "You can call me Madame Angler or just Madame." She elaborates that the microwave is no loss as they are not allowed at the St. George. He must follow two rules: "Don't hang pictures on the wall with nails. If you must put something up, use tape." She also says he will be expected to deposit all "organic" leftovers and trash in the disposal regularly.

As soon as Madame Angler and the maintenance workers leave, Archie starts violating the first rule. He bangs a nail into a wall. As he hammers, a loud growl is heard. He hangs up a photograph of his mother. But it soon crashes on the floor, followed by the nail that held it up. Then the wall bleeds.

In a later scene, Archie is astonished to watch how much food Madame Angler throws down the disposal. She explains it as a dislike of leftovers and then takes him to task for not putting much organic garbage down the disposal.

It turns out that the secret of St. George is that the apartment complex is itself alive, an organism that must be regularly fed to stay alive. No monster need creep up on the characters in this episode. They live inside the monster.

Throughout the episode, Marie delivers a deliberately over-the-top performance as the creepy and twisted Madame Angler. In keeping with the show's trademark fusing of horror with comedy, Marie resembles Vincent Price (in most of his performances) in acting in a tongue-in-cheek manner. Perhaps her best moment is at the end when one of the maintenance workers gripes that Archie was "especially hard to stomach" and she releases a boisterously extended witch's cackle.

During the 1980s, when Marie was in her sixties, she began suffering very serious health problems. "Mom had a heart attack in her sixties," Rick Hupp remembered. He elaborated that doctors believed the heart attack was linked to her smoking habit. "She quit smoking promptly after the heart attack," he related. "She had been smoking since she was fourteen, and tried numerous times to quit, but just couldn't until the heart attack scared her into quitting," he continued.

The latter part of 1985 saw Marie join with many other prominent performers in a project designed to help the less fortunate. A *Los Angeles Times* piece published in late November reported that May Company, together with a charity called LIFE that aimed to "fight hunger," held a drive in which people were invited to donate "non-perishable food" items "until Christmas." On a designated Saturday such donors could "trade food for a photo with the stars at May Company." Other entertainment luminaries besides Marie who participated included Joe Lawrence, Dennis Weaver, Lee Meriwether, Harvey Norman, Marty Angels, Alejandro Rey, Ed Begley Jr., and Beverly Garland.

Marie never lost what she called the "pioneer spirit" that kept her trying to meet the next goal. In a 1985 interview, she told the reporter that a plaque graced her home bearing the maxim, "Today is the first day of the rest of your life." She added of that maxim, "I'm guided by it and that's how I like to play this most enjoyable game of life."

In another 1985 interview, Marie discussed how SAG was riven by disputes about the direction it should take. For about ten years, Marie said, there had been dispute within the organization as to how politicized it should be. Marie sided with those like Charlton Heston and Burt Reynolds who believed SAG should steer clear of general political issues. *Daily Herald* writer Laura Jones reported that this faction "resented union dues being spent in support of various liberal causes including the air controllers strike." Jones quoted Marie: "We wanted our union to get back to its original purpose which was tending to the business of actors' wages, working conditions, pensions, and welfare—period." Marie contended that SAG President Ed Asner was voted into office more because of the popularity of his TV show *Lou Grant* rather than his views. "When his motives and plans for using the union to forward his own ideals became apparent, most people backed off," she elaborated. Asner, and performers such as Patty Duke, believed SAG should merge with the Screen Extras Guild. "It wasn't that those of us who opposed them didn't believe in collective bargaining," Marie said. "We did and we still do. But we didn't want to be part of a big labor movement." The SAG Board of Directors took a vote on the question of the merger. Jones reports, "When the ballots were tallied, there was one that opposed the action. Only one but that was enough. Windsor's vote, in effect, won time for those who disagreed with Asner to band together and form AWAG—Actors Working for an Actor's Guild." Marie worked with others to keep SAG out of politics. "At the time of the last elections, there were 13 seats on the board available," Marie noted. "People affiliated with AWAG won 12 of them so the pendulum is beginning to swing in our direction."

The year 1986 saw Marie on the stage in Hollywood in a play entitled *The Bar Off Melrose*. The old saying "too many cooks spoil the broth" does not appear to apply to this play in which no less than fifteen authors collaborated to craft the script. What's more, they created a play for no less than forty performers! Directed by Bill Court, it was very well-received. The setting is, not surprising, a bar located off Melrose. "It shows different segments of different people's lives," Marie explained. "Bill Court will amaze you by his cleverness of manipulating forty actors on and off the stage." What is it about? "It's about everything," Marie said. "There's something for everyone." Tickets sold out and it got glowing reviews. She played a has-been actress who found solace in alcohol. Her character tried for a comeback in a play. Marie's performance led to a Los Angeles Drama Critics Award for Best Actress in 1987.

Marie's last appearance in a motion picture made for release in theaters was in the 1987 *Commando Squad,* a pretty run-of-the-mill action flick starring former *Playboy* Playmate Kathy Shower as super-duper gun-slinging and martial arts expert Kat Withers, a narcotics agent who travels to Mexico to bring down a bunch of drug smugglers. It is also personal as the gang kidnaps the man she wants. Although the credits read "Also Starring Marie Windsor," Marie was only in a single scene and her part was a bit. Marie played Casey, the owner of a memorabilia store—a business that served as a front for unlawful doings. She is behind the counter when a child customer asks for a movie poster. Perhaps the screenwriter makes a reference to Marie's lower-list fame when she cheerfully observes, "All you kids like Z-grade movies." Kat walks in. It is obvious the two know each other when Kat requests "party favors." Casey places a "We Are Gone" sign at the front of her store so she and her special client can do their business behind it. Casey slips from routine chat about her grandkids to showing off her cache of illegal weapons such as grenades and a hollowed-out knife filled with sulfuric acid. Marie easily slides from workaday cashier to cold-blooded weapons dealer.

That same year of 1987 saw her in two TV series episodes: "For Old Crime's Sake" on *Simon & Simon* and "The Cemetery Vote" on *Murder, She Wrote.* In 1988, she played a character named Billie Costello on the television series *Supercarrier.* Her second to last TV appearance was in 1990 on *The New Adam-12.* She later relayed an interesting experience from working on that show. "We were working on location in the Valley [Burbank] using a little stucco house in a very inexpensive area," Marie recalled. "The lady who owned the house graciously let me come in to change my wardrobe." That woman asked, "Did you know this is the house where Oliver Hardy died?" Marie had not known. "She took me to the room where he had spent his last days." When she worked on that show, she also worked with star Ethan Wayne, a son of John Wayne.

It was about this time that Marie underwent her third, and last, facelift.

Marie's very last television appearance took place on a *Murder, She Wrote* episode that aired on February 10, 1991. The episode was entitled "Who Killed J.B. Fletcher?" Perhaps it was appropriate that this episode reunited Marie with other performers from her Golden Age of Hollywood heyday including Jane Withers, Terry Moore, Margaret O'Brien, Janet Blair, Betty Garrett, and, of course, series star Angela Lansbury. Max Baer, Jr., who achieved his greatest glory as the endearingly silly Jethro Bodine of *The Beverly Hillbillies* in the 1960s, also had a small part in this episode. "Who Killed J.B. Fletcher?" was not only Marie's cinematic swan song but that of Janet Blair as well. Indeed, the overall casting of the episode makes it, as noted by an IMDb reviewer, "an episode for nostalgia lovers."

A famous, if inaccurate, quote attributed to Mark Twain, "reports of my death have been greatly exaggerated," is appropriate for this TV episode. The episode commences with Marge Allen (Jane Withers), decked out in a classic cowboy/girl hat, pretending to be famed mystery writer Jessica Fletcher as she finds her way after office hours into the office of the McCauley dog kennel. "Hold it there, ma'am," a police officer admonishes. Marge is arrested and identifies herself as Fletcher. Since she possesses identification that appears official, she is booked and bailed out as Fletcher. It turns out she used the false identity because she is the mother of a senator and wants to avoid embroiling him in scandal. Once bailed out, she goes to the McCauley home where she is greeted by Lisa McCauley, a lovely young woman whose head is graced by a cascading mane of red curls. She turns around and sees something that puts terror on her face.

Jessica Fletcher is shocked to learn that "mystery writer Jessica Fletcher" had been busted in a town called Bremerton for breaking and entering into a dog kennel office. She phones Bremerton law enforcement to protest that she was not the one arrested. The town's sheriff scoffs at her so she decides she must make an appearance there to straighten things out.

When she is in the police department, she has trouble convincing Sheriff J.T. Tanner (Earl Holliman) that she, not the arrestee, is the true Jessica Fletcher. She eventually manages to get the point across with a picture on the back of one of her books.

Since Jessica Fletcher is in the town, and since she is a natural investigator, she wants to find out who it was who pretended to be her. It does not take long before she finds herself at a meeting of a very relevant local group: The Jessica Fletcher Literary Society. The entire club is formed of "Golden Girls" of about Fletcher's vintage—including Caroline, whom Marie plays. Why would Marge Allen have realistic looking identification as Fletcher? "My family runs a little print shop so I had them make up Jessica Fletcher I.D. cards just for fun," Marie-as-Caroline cheerfully explains. Fletcher asks that they destroy them and their respect for her is such that they easily submit to her wishes.

Not too long after this, Fletcher picks up a newspaper with a headline saying she is dead! Of course, it is the fake Fletcher, Marge, who is dead—apparently killed in a car accident. Soon after this, we learn that the male half of the McCauley kennel owning team has been killed in an apparent hunting accident.

Since accidental deaths are rarely what they seem on any detective show, our heroine is on the trail to find the truth. This episode is chock full of appropriate twists and turns before Jessica Fletcher (the real one) ties all the clues together at the end. Marie's part was small but, as usual, she handled it well, making her participation in this a worthwhile finale to a distinguished acting career.

In an interview she gave in 1991, Marie looked back on her career and commented on how frequently (but by no means always) she was called upon to play characters who were… well, lacking in good character. "Playing heavies is fun and the parts usually have meatier dialogue to chew on," she remarked. She continued that there were time when she "wanted to be Greer Garson" and "play things like Mrs. Miniver." However, she believed she was rarely cast in such roles due to her appearance: "My height has always handicapped me. And my 'look' with my prominent eyes. I look more like the madam of a brothel than I do the girl next door!" She laughed at the observation. It should be noted that there were times when she played "next door" types and did well playing them. The loving wife and concerned mother she played in *The Day Mars Invaded Earth* is a good example of Marie as a wholesome and sympathetic character.

30

The Sunset Years, Death, Legacy

A 1992 *FILMFAX* MAGAZINE FEATURED an interview Marie gave to Mark A. Miller in which she talked about her movie career. Even in her golden years, she felt acting "comes with its many rewards, not the least of which is to help me stay younger and be more stimulating to myself and others."

She did eventually stop acting in the 1990s. Retiring from acting hardly meant that the life of this "seasoned citizen" was idle. She was still a wife as well as stepmom and mom to two adults. Always artistic, she now had more time to give over to those pursuits. A side of the garage at her residence was a small artist studio in which she kept paint, paintbrushes, an easel, and other supplies for painting. What were her favorite subjects to paint? "She painted great bowls of fruit, landscapes—especially Utah landscapes—and sometimes people," Rick Hupp said. She also crafted pottery.

"I also have some recall about my mom running an art gallery for a few years out of dad's real estate office in Beverly Hills," Hupp stated. "She was industrious!"

In Marie's 70s, her health began to seriously decline. She struggled with arthritis and with problems in her eyes as well as with her heart. One problem was related to her three facelifts. "She began having eye dryness problems," Rick Hupp disclosed. "When she slept her eyes did not close all the way, and the doctors determined that her face had been pulled back enough times that it inhibited her eyelids from covering her eyes completely when she slept."

Unrelated to the facelifts, on one awful morning, she work up and realized that she had lost most of the sight in one eye. "She experienced a lot of grief over that at first, but then she just seemed to adapt to it," Rick said.

"She really didn't spend much time complaining about her ailments. She prided herself as a can do person, and I don't remember her ever acting like a victim. Would she advocate for her needs and relief—yes! But never as a victim. It's interesting to see the same assertiveness she practiced in real life portrayed in many of her characters."

A problem also occurred with one of the breast implants that had been put in her in the 1970s in reconstructive surgery. "Some sort of infection occurred near one of the implants and it was removed," Rick stated. "This chronic infection really took its toll on her. It sapped her energy, and it took quite awhile for the doctors to figure out why her blood tests kept coming back showing she had an infection somewhere in her body. On a hunch, the doctors did some exploratory surgery to see what they couldn't detect with X-rays and discovered that there was an infection behind one of the implants. As soon as they removed it, her vitality returned rapidly!"

Although she was no longer acting, the woman who had contributed so much to the entertainment industry was hardly forgotten by the public. Fans continued to write to Marie Windsor to let her know how much her varied performances were appreciated. In an interview granted in her 70s, she said that most fan letters commented on her performances in *The Narrow Margin* and *The Killing*. About the attention she continued to receive, Marie commented, "For [an] actress who… never became a genuine name-above-the-title star, there's consolation in belated recognition."

During the summer of 1993, Turner Classic Movies (TCM) honored four still-living actresses of film noir on cable TV. Those four were Marie, Audrey Totter, Colleen Gray, and Jane Greer. The foursome gathered one afternoon at Formosa Café, a Hollywood eatery that became well-known during the heyday of these actresses, in August of the same year to reminisce about the work being showcased by TCM. Audrey Totter, famed for *Lady in the Lake* (1946), *The Postman Always Rings Twice* (1946), *The Set-Up* (1949), and *Tension* (1950), cheerfully disclosed, "These films are very big all over Europe, and lately Eastern Europe, and I still get mail asking if I'm married. They have no idea that I'm a grandmother now!"

Colleen Gray's film noir career was different than that of the other three because she typically played virtuous characters. "The bad girls were so much fun to play!" Totter said. "I wouldn't have wanted to play Colleen's good girl parts." "Who would?" Colleen chirped, adding, "Like in *The Killing*, I was the good girl. It was very frustrating. And Marie had the big, fat, juicy part."

"They [bad characters] were always the most fun to play," Marie readily agreed. As much as she relished playing "bad" characters, Marie's moral and social conservatism showed in her analysis of what made film noir great, arguing that rules forbidding explicit sex helped fuel audience imagination. "Everything was implied but not shown," Marie stated. "Film noir engaged the audience, let them use the gray matter between their ears."

In December 1993, a newspaper of Wilkes-Barre, Pennsylvania, *Citizens Voice*, ran an article about holiday recipes used by stars. The piece featured "Bing Crosby's Christmas Venison," "Frank Petty's Polenta with Game Sauce," and "Marie Windsor's Mincemeat Pie A La Etta Bertelsen." At the end of the article, reporter Johna Blinn states that Marie Windsor's recipe "is from her mother, Etta Bertelsen." The article was illustrated with a photograph of a smiling Marie at a table, knife and fork cutting into a meal. The recipe was said to make a dessert that "serves 6 to 8." It went as follows.

> 1 jar (18 ounces) prepared mincemeat
> 1 ½ cup walnuts, coarsely broken
> 2 large apples, washed, diced
> ½ cup packed brown sugar
> ¼ cup brandy or rum
> 1 tablespoon lemon juice
> 1 prepared pastry for 2-crust, 9-inch pie

Day before, in medium-size mixing bowl, combine mincemeat, walnuts, apples, sugar, brandy and lemon juice; stir until well mixed. Cover, refrigerate overnight to allow flavors to blend. Three hours before serving, roll out half the pastry. Line a 9-inch pie plate; fill pastry shell with undrained mincemeat mixture. Prepare top crust as for a lattice topping. Fold pastry strips over lower crust; pinch with fingers to seal. Bake in preheated 425 F. oven 30 to 40 minutes until golden. Serve warm with hard sauce or cream cheese.

The newspaper stated in an "afterthought" that "hard sauce" could be "made from ½ cup butter creamed together with 2 cups confectioner's sugar, flavored with 1 teaspoon vanilla extract or rum or brandy." It estimated that the forgoing would make about 1 2/3 cups.

During the mid-to-late 1990s, arthritis increasingly caused Marie severe pain as well as—literally—cramping her style. Her arthritis led to a series of surgical operations starting in 1996. She underwent a back operation on June 2, 1997 that left Marie paralyzed. "My third or fourth lumbar was like a rat's nest," she said. However, the paralysis was not permanent. "After extensive surgery, I can drive and walk with a cane," she added in an interview for a book published in 1999.

Plagued by health problems as she was, Marie continued living an active life. In August 1999, Hollywood's Egyptian Theatre ran *The Narrow Margin* for a week and followed it with a week of *The Killing*. "I attended the screenings, then answered questions afterwards, followed by a long autograph session," she said. "It was very rewarding!"

She was at home on December 10, 2000 when congestive heart failure ended Marie Windsor's life. It was only one day shy of what would have been her 81st birthday. She left Jack Hupp a widower.

Marie also left behind an impressive body of work. She was a significant figure in the creation of the movie genre now known as film noir. Her motion pictures include such widely respected classics as *Force of Evil*, *The Killing*, and *The Narrow Margin*. Marie did excellent and varied work on the stage and in radio and television.

In October 2001, a painting she had done was purchased at an estate sale at her Beverly Hills home. The small painting measured about 6 inches high and five inches wide displayed a representation of a potted plant and was signed "M.W." in a corner.

A drawing depicting Marie by artist Ronda A. West began being displayed on the Star Portraits website in 2018. The drawing shows Marie as she was at the height of her fame, hair around her in dark waves, the slightest of smiles playing on her lips, and those lovely eyes looking wisely at the viewer.

It is likely every performer in Hollywood yearns for superstar status. Marie succinctly put this wish into perspective as applied to her career: "Sure, I'm sad I've never made it to being a big superstar but I feel absolutely no bitterness. I came out of a town of 250 people and what I've done is extraordinary."

Indeed it is. The author of this biography hopes this book is a tribute to the extraordinary accomplishments, indeed, the extraordinary life, of Marie Windsor.

Bibliography

"3 Films Have Premieres: Kathryn Grayson Portrays Grace Moore in 'So This Is Love' at the Normandie." *The New York Times*. Aug. 12, 1953.

"Abbott and Costello Mark Milestone in Current Film." *The Bristol Herald Courier*. July 3, 1955.

"Abbott and Costello Meet the Mummy." (1955). *Internet Movie Database*.

"Actress." *Palm Beach Daily News*. June 1, 1989

"African Sequences Really Shot There." *The Los Angeles Times*. May 10, 1949.

"Amusements." *The Post-Star*. Oct. 10, 1950.

Anderson, Nancy. "No Gables in Hollywood, says Marie Windsor." *The Danville News*. May 24, 1973.

Arnold, Jeremy. "Trouble Along the Way." *TCM.com*.

Batman: "Green Ice" 1966.http://nummtheory.blogspot.com/2020/08/batman-green-ice-1966.html.

B.C. "At Loew's State." *The New York Times*. Dec. 27, 1948.

"A New Lease On Life." (1986). *Tales from the Darkside. Internet Movie Database*.

"Appleby's Bearded Boarder." March 6, 1965. *The Red Skelton Hour. Internet Movie Database*.

A. W. "Sagebrush Opera, Minus Cattle." *The New York Times*. Sept. 19, 1949.

Baxter, John. *Stanley Kubrick: A Biography.* Carroll & Graf Publishers, Inc. New York. 1997.

"Beautiful 'Y' Coeds Vie For Carnival Queen Honors." *The Daily Herald.*

"Belle Starr." (1954). *Stories of the Century. Internet Movie Database.*

Benny, Mary Livingston; Marks, Hilliard; and Borie, Marcia. *Jack Benny.* Doubleday & Company, Inc.

Bergan, Ronald. "Marie Windsor." *The Guardian.* Jan. 23, 2001.

Berges, Marshall. "Marie Windsor & Jack Hupp." *The Los Angeles Times.* Oct. 28, 1973.

Bernstein, Adam. "Prolific B-Movie Star Marie Windsor Dies." *The Washington Post.* Dec. 14, 2000.

Betancourt, John Edward. "'Tales from the Darkside' Retro Recap: 'A New Lease on Life.'" *Nerds that Geek.*

"Bill Brackets Fire and C-Man." *The Los Angeles Times.*

Blinn, Johna. "A good meal must be served properly, says actress Windsor." *Clarion-Ledger.* Dec. 27, 1979.

Blinn, Johna. "Best holiday recipes used by stars perfect for year-end entertaining." *Citizens Voice.* Dec. 4, 1993.

Blinn, Johna. "Crystal is part of fine dining." *The Ithaca Journal.* Dec. 21, 1979.

"The Bounty Hunter." (1954). *Internet Movie Database.*

Butler, Craig. *Story of Mankind. allmovie.com.*

"B.Y.U. Girl Crowned Queen of S. L. Covered Wagon Days." *The Daily Herald.*

"Cahill: United States Marshal (1973)." *At-A-Glance Film Reviews.*

"Cahill: United States Marshal (1973)." *Internet Movie Database.*

"Cahill: United States Marshal." *TCM.com.*

Canby, Vincent. "Film: 'Cahill, United States Marshal' Stars Wayne." *The New York Times.* July 12, 1973.

Canby, Vincent. "Film Festival: Nostalgia: 'Hearts of the West' Views Early 30's Hollywood." *The New York Times.* Oct. 4. 1975.

"The Case of the Daring Decoy." (1958). *Perry Mason. Internet Movie Database.*

"The Case of the Wednesday Woman." (1964). *Perry Mason. Internet Movie Database.*

"The Case of the Madcap Modiste." (1960). *Perry Mason. Internet Movie Database.*

"The Case of the Tarnished Trademark." (1962). *Perry Mason. Internet Movie Database.*

"Cat-Women of the Moon." *Encyclopedia of Science Fiction.*

Cat-Women of the Moon. Variety.

"Cauliflower's Hamburger Stand." (1958). *The Red Skelton Hour. Internet Movie Database.*

"Chamber of Horrors." *TCM.com.*

"Chamber of Horrors." (1966). *Internet Movie Database.*

Chennault, Nicholas. *The Showdown.* March 25, 2014. *Thegreatwesternmovies.com.*

"City That Never Sleeps." (1958). *Internet Movie Database.*

"City That Never Sleeps." *Lansing State Journal.* Aug. 8, 1953.

"City That Never Sleeps." *TCM.com.*

"City That Never Sleeps." *Variety.*

Clary, Patricia. "Hollywood Film Shop." *The Terre Haute Tribune.*

"Coming to Salt Lake." *Deseret News.* June 6, 1949.

"Commando Squad." (1987). *Internet Movie Database.*

Crowther, Brosley. "At Loew's State." *New York Times.* Dec. 27, 1948.

"'Dakota Lil' and 'Boy from Indiana' on double program at 'New Ames.'" *Ames Daily Tribune.* June 3, 1950.

"'Dakota Lil' at the Imperial." *The Gazette.* June 10, 1950.

"Dakota Lil." (1950). *Internet Movie Database.*

"Dakota Lil." *TCM.com.*

"Dakota Lil." *Variety.* Jan. 20, 1950.

"The Day Mars Invaded Earth." (1962). *Internet Movie Database.*

"The Day Mars Invaded Earth." *TCM.com.*

"The Day Mars Invaded Earth." https://moviesandmania.com/2018/11/09/
the-day-mars-invaded-earth-usa-1963/

"Day of the Badman." (1958). *Internet Movie Database.*

"Deadeye and the Magician." (1960). *The Red Skelton Hour. Internet Movie Database.*

"Deep Freeze." (1960). *Batman. Internet Movie Database.*

Deming, Mark. Synopsis *Story of Mankind. allmovie.com.*

"Double Deal." *Dennis Schwartz Movie Reviews.*

"Double Deal." (1950). *Internet Movie Database.*

"Double Deal." *The Cincinnati Enquirer.* July 23, 1950.

"Double Deal." *TCM.com.*

"'Double Deal' May Star Stage Actor." *The Los Angeles Times.* May 29, 1950.

Ebert, Roger. "A heist played like a game of chess." *RogerEbert.com.*

Ebert, Roger. "Hearts of the West." *RogerEbert.com.*

"The Eddie Cantor Story." *TCM.com.*

Erickson, Glenn. *"Chamber of Horrors." TCM.com.*

"Fatal Fraud." (1954). *The Whistler. Internet Movie Database.*

"Fighting Kentuckian." (1949). *Internet Movie Database.*

"Film Bill Presented in Varied Dimensions." *The Los Angeles Times.* April
18, 1953.

"Film Noir Actress Marie Windsor Estate Item Painting." https://www.
worthpoint.com/worthopedia/film-noir-actress-marie-wind-
sor-20990872

Fitzgerald, Michael G.; Magers, Boyd. *Ladies of the Western: Interviews with Fifty-One More Actresses from the Silent Era to the Television Westerns of the 1950s and 1960s.* McFarland & Company, Inc., Publishers. Jefferson, North Carolina, and London. 1999.

"For the record." *The Los Angeles Times.* Jan. 31, 1983.

"Force of Evil." Turner Classic Movies. https://www.tcm.com/tcmdb/title/75384/force-of-evil/#overview.

"Force of Evil." American Film Institute.

"Force of Evil (1948). *Internet Movie Database.*

Fox, Fred W. "'Frenchie' Girls Stage Wild Brawl." *The Mirror.* Dec. 26, 1950.

"Freddie and the Brooklyn Dodgers." (1957). *The Red Skelton Hour. Internet Movie Database.*

"Freddie and the Millionaire." (1958). *The Red Skelton Hour. Internet Movie Database.*

"Frenchie." (1950). *Internet Movie Database.*

"Frenchie." *TCM.com.*

"'Frenchie' Part 2." *Chicago Daily Tribune.* Nov. 24, 1950.

Gerald, Joe Fitz. "City That Never Sleeps." *The Lincoln Star.* Oct. 25, 1953.

"The Girl in Black Stockings." *TCM.com.*

"The Girl in Black Stockings." (1957). *Classic Movie Ramblings.*

"The Girl in Black Stockings." (1957). *Internet Movie Database.*

"Governor Gets Monogram Pix." *The Billboard.* Oct. 1, 1955.

"The Great Brain Robbery." (1961). *The Red Skelton Hour. Internet Movie Database.*

"Green Ice." 1966. *Batman. Internet Movie Database.*

Hagen, Ray; Wagner, Laura. *Killer Tomatoes: Fifteen Tough Film Dames.* McFarland & Company, Inc. 2004.

Hal. "Film Review: *Hellfire* (1949). *The Horn Section.*

Hale, Wanda. "George Montgomery in Palace Western." *Daily News.* March 3, 1950.

"Hearts of the West." (1975). Internet Movie Database.

Hellfire (1949). *Internet Movie Database.*

"Hell's Half Acre." (1954). Internet Movie Database.

"Hellfire." (1949). The Marie Windsor Blogathon.

H. H. T. "At the Rialto." *The New York Times.* March 20, 1954.

"High Lonesome Country." (1972). *Alias Smith and Jones. Internet Movie Database.*

"Hollywood." (1979). *Lou Grant. Internet Movie Database.*

"Hollywood." *Radio Daily.* July 5, 1949.

"Hollywood Welcome." *The Los Angeles Times.* Aug. 23, 1947.

"Hurricane Island (1951)." *Fantastic Movie Musings and Ramblings.*

"Hurricane Island." (1951). *Internet Movie Database.*

"Incident of the Painted Lady." (1961). *Rawhide. Internet Movie Database.*

"India's Hollywood Takeaway." *The Wayback Machine.*

"Jack Carson & Marie Windsor Star in 'Johnny Come Lately.'" *The Times-Mail.* Aug. 6, 1960.

"Japanese War Bride." (1952). *Internet Movie Database.*

"Jon Hall Discovers Costume Role Heavy Going in Tropical Weather." *The Gazette.* Aug. 27, 1951.

Jones, Laura. "Actress Played Major Role in Battle Raging Within Screen Actors' Guild." *The Daily Herald.* Aug. 18, 1985.

"The Jungle." (1952). *Internet Movie Database.*

"The Jungle." *TCM.com.*

Jones, Laura. "From Miss Utah to 'Wasted Queen' of B Flicks." *The Daily Herald.* Aug. 18, 1985.

"The Killing." Criterion Collection.

"The Killing." (1956). *Internet Movie Database.*

"The Killing." *Variety.* 6/18/1956.

"'Little Big Horn' Tells Intense Story of Custer." *The Courier-Journal.* July 13, 1951.

"Little Cabbage." Nov. 27, 1960. *Internet Movie Database.*

"Limerick Contest Winners to See 'The Tall Texan.'" *Denton Record-Chronicle.* March 15, 1953.

"Little Big Horn." (1951). *Internet Movie Database.*

"Little Big Horn (Good)." *The Tidings.* July 27, 1951.

"Love is Feeding Everyone." *The Los Angeles Times.* Nov. 28, 1985.

"Lovely but Deadly." (1981). *Internet Movie Database.*

"Manhunter." (1974). *Internet Movie Database.*

"Marie Windsor." *Internet Movie Database.*

"Marie Windsor: A Sheep in Wolf's Clothing." *Travalanche.* Dec. 11, 2018.

"Marie Windsor: A Shining Light." *Utah's Piute County.*

"Marie Windsor: A Sheep in Wolf's Clothing." https://travsd.wordpress.com/2018/12/11/marie-windsor-a-sheep-in-wolfs-clothing/

"Marie Windsor Collection." https://www.otrcat.com/p/marie-windsor

"Marie Windsor Back at Work." *Los Angeles Evening Citizen News.* June 6, 1963.

"Marie Windsor, Area's Own Star, Honored." *The Richfield Reaper.* Feb. 2, 1983.

"Marie Windsor gets her star." *Fort Worth Star-Telegram.* Jan. 20, 1983.

"Marie Windsor: Her Face Is Familiar." *Lubbock Avalanche-Journal.*

"Marie Windsor in 'Bonanza.'" *The Ithaca Journal.* May 21, 1966.

"Marie Windsor Quotes." *Quotepark.com.*

"Marie Windsor Rivals Betty Grable." *The Los Angeles Times.* Jan. 5, 1949.

"Marie Windsor to be on Lyric Stage for Two Days." *Deseret News*. June 6, 1949.

"Marie Windsor." *TCM.com*.

"Marie Windsor." *Torgo the White's Rolodex*.

"Marie Windsor." *Western Clippings*.

"Marie Windsor Quotes." *Quotes of Famous People*.

"Marysvale Girl Wins Role In Jack Benny Movie." *The Salt Lake Tribune*. April 23, 1942.

Meyer, Jim. "'Support Your Gunfighter' Skillfully Handled Farce." *Tallahassee Democrat*. July 28, 1971.

"Midnight." *News-Pilot*. Nov. 5, 1982.

"Milk Creek comedy classics #71: 'Smart Alecks' (1942)." *Dead 2 Rights*.

"Mystery of the Green Feather." (1972). *Her Ramsey. Internet Movie Database*.

"The Narrow Margin." (1952). *Internet Movie Database*.

"The Narrow Margin." *TCM.com*.

Nehme, Farran Smith. "Restorations from Republic Pictures Reveal a Studio That Got Its Hands Dirty." *The Village Voice*. Feb. 6, 2018.

"New Abbott and Costello Comedy Is Hilarious Film." *Caspar Star-Tribune*. July 20, 1955.

"New Films 'Dallas' At Strand Theater." *Hartford Courant*. Dec. 29, 1950.

Newton. "Spotlight On: Imperial Universal Studios Mummy Figure." *infinitehollywood.com*.

"Nine-Day Wonder." *Clovis News-Journal*. Aug. 21, 1950.

Nixon, Rob. "Abbott and Costello Meet the Mummy." *TCM.com*.

Nail, John. "No Matter How You Spell It." *Taste Is No Object*.

"New Abbott and Costello Comedy is Hilarious Film." *Caspar-Star Tribune*. July 20, 1955.

"Noir-vember 2015: No Man's Woman." *Martin Teller's Movie Reviews.* Nov. 12, 2015.

"No Man's Woman (1955)." *Internet Movie Database.*

"No Matter How You Spell It." *Taste Is No Object.*

"Not Much Time." *The Los Angeles Times.* Nov. 7, 1946.

"The Outfit." (1973). *Internet Movie Database.*

"Outlaw Women." Dennis Schwartz Movie Reviews.

"Outlaw Women." (1952). *Internet Movie Database.*

"Outlaw Women." *TCM.com.*

Padgitt, James. "In Hollywood." *Tyrone Daily Herald.* June 27, 1950.

"Palace Presents Murder Thriller." *The New York Times.* Feb. 27, 1954.

"'Pantomime Quiz Time'—Misc 1954 Episode." https://archive.org/details/PantomimeQuiz1954

"Paradise Alley." (1962). *Internet Movie Database.*

"Paradise Alley." *Letterboxd—Your life in film.*

Parker, Ben S. "Fighting Featuring Women Enlivens Strand's New Film." *The Commercial Appeal.* May 9, 1956.

"The Perfect Woman." *Balladeer's Blog.*

"The Perfect Woman." (1981). *Internet Movie Database.*

"The Perfect Woman." *Reviewing Every TV Show I Own.*

"The Picnic." June 2, 1956. *The Red Skelton Hour. Internet Movie Database.*

"Ponce de Leon's Search Backgrounds New Movie." *Orlando Evening Star.* Oct. 22, 1951.

"Premiere Set Here Here For 'Japanese War Bride,' Film Made in Salinas." *The Californian.* Feb. 8, 1952.

"The Rebel." (1960). *Glory. Internet Movie Database.*

Renshaw, Jerry. "Marie Windsor Tales of Noir and Be Movies." *The Austin Chronicle.* Oct. 31, 1997.

"Remembrance of Things Past—*Scarecrow and Mrs. King*." 1984. *Internet Movie Database*.

"The Ring." Aug. 23, 1954. *Public Defender. Internet Movie Database*.

"Salem's Lot." *TimeOut*.

"San Fernando's Showboat." (1957). *The Red Skelton Hour. Internet Movie Database*.

"Scarecrow and Mrs. King." *allmovie.com*.

Scheuer, Phillip K. "Patrol in Heroic Try to Warn Custer at Horn." *The Los Angeles Times*. July 12, 1951.

"School Gives Out Diplomas." *The Salt Lake Tribune*.

Scott, John L. "'Japanese War Bride' Arrives On Screens." *The Los Angeles Times*. Feb. 8, 1952.

Screen Scout. "'Frenchie' One of Better Westerns." *The San Francisco Examiner*. Dec. 26, 1951.

"Screen to Claim 1939 Covered Wagon Days Queen." *The Salt Lake Tribune*. Oct. 23, 1940.

"Seance/The Treasure." (1979). *Fantasy Island. Internet Movie Database*.

"Shelley Winters and Joel McCrea Are Co-Starred in 'Frenchie.'" *Messenger-Inquirer*. Dec. 24, 1950.

"Sideshow." (1980). *The Incredible Hulk. Internet Movie Database*.

"The Showdown." (1950). *Internet Movie Database*.

"The Showdown." (1950). *TCM.com*.

"Smart Alecks." (1942). *At-A-Glance Film Reviews*.

"Smart Alecks." (1941). *Internet Movie Database*.

"'Smart Alecks' Previewed. *Los Angeles Times*. June 22, 1942.

"So This Is Love." (1953). *Internet Movie Database*.

"Song of the Thin Man." (1947). *Internet Movie Database*.

"Space Thriller Booked." *Standard-Speaker*. April 26, 1963.

"Stage Show and Film at Earle." *The Philadelphia Inquirer*. Sept. 7, 1951.

"Star No. 1,758 to Marie Windsor." *The Los Angeles Times*. Jan. 22, 1983.

"Staunton Movie Talk." *The Daily News Leader*. Oct. 4, 1955.

Stein, Ruthie. "*Force of Evil*." DVD Reviews.

Story of Mankind. (1957). *Internet Movie Database*.

"*Story of Mankind* Unravels at Paramount." *The New York Times*. Nov. 9, 1957.

"Stump the Stars." (1954). *Internet Movie Database*.

"Support Your Local Gunfighter." (1971). Internet Movie Database.

"Swamp Women/Swamp Diamonds/Cruel Swamp." (1955). ww.1000misspenthours.com/reviews/reviewsn-z/swampwomen.htm

"Swamp Diamonds (1956). B&S About Movies.

"Swamp Women." (1956). *Internet Movie Database*.

"Swamp Women." (1955). *Filmfanatic.org*

Swindell, Larry. *Body and Soul: The Story of John Garfield*. William Morrow and Company, Inc. New York. 1975.

"The Tall Texan." (1953). *Internet Movie Database*.

"Tall Texan Packed with Emotions." *The Salt Lake Tribune*. June 10, 1953.

"The Tall Texan." (1953). *Snakes in Movies*.

"The Tall Texan." *TCM.com*.

"Taylor Holmes in 'Double Deal.'" *Valley Times*. July 27, 1950.

Thomson, David. "Was This the Most Dangerous Film in American History?" *New Republic*. July 29, 2012.

"Thumbnail Reviews." *Mirror News*. Feb. 21, 1950.

"Tonight's Movie: Double Deal (1950)." *Laura's Miscellaneous Musings*.

"Tonight's Movie: No Man's Woman (1955)—An Olive Films DVD Review." *Laura's Miscellaneous Musings*.

"Taylor Holmes in 'Double Deal.'" *Valley Times*. July 27, 1950.

"Trouble Along the Way." (1953). *Internet Movie Database.*

"Trouble Along the Way." *Variety.*

"Two-Dollar Bettor." (1951). *Internet Movie Database.*

"Two-Dollar Bettor." *Dennis Schwartz Movie Reviews.*

"Two-Dollar Bettor." *Martin Teller's Movie Reviews.*

"Utah Native Gets Star on Walk of Fame." *The Salt Lake Tribune.* Jan. 21, 1983.

"Warmly, Marie Windsor." *stephenbwhatley.com.*

Welsh, Mark David. "The Jungle." (1952).

Weinraub, Bernard. "Film noir star: 'Bad girls were so much fun to play.'" *The Atlanta Constitution.* Aug. 25, 1999.

"Who Killed J.B. Fletcher?" *Murder, She Wrote. Internet Movie Database.*

Wild Women. (1970 TV Movie). *Internet Movie Database.*

Yablonsky, Lewis. *George Raft.* Mercury House, Incorporated. 1989.